FLORIDA

Civics

Guided Reading Workbook

Houghton Mifflin Harcourt

Printed in the U.S.A.

ISBN 978-0-544-82617-5

7 8 9 10 0928 25 24 23 22 21 20 19

4500753327 A B C D E F G

Contents

The Citizen in Society

The American Economy

The United States and the World

How to Use this Book

The *Guided Reading Workbook* was developed to help you get the most from your reading. Using this book will help you master United States civics content while developing your reading and vocabulary skills. Reviewing the next few pages before getting started will make you aware of the many useful features in this book.

Section summary pages allow you to interact with the content and key terms from each section of a chapter. The summaries explain each section of your textbook in a way that is easy to understand.

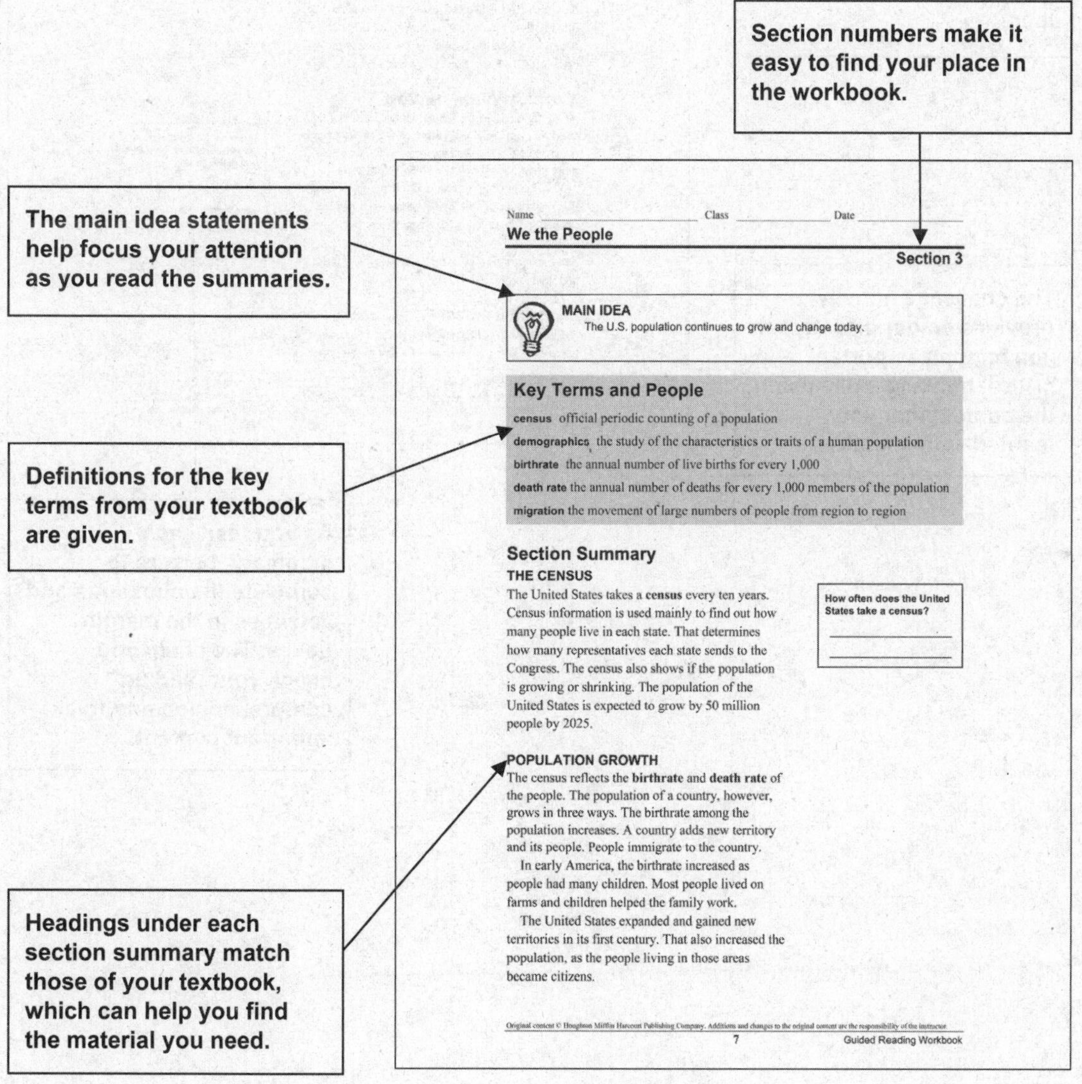

Name ____________ Class ________ Date ________

Section 3, *continued*

The immigration of people from other countries also added to the population. Since 1820, more than 60 million people have come to the United States.

POPULATION CHANGES

Information collected in the census tells us the **demographics** of the U.S. population. Lifestyles change, and the census shows us those changes. The number of people in each household and whether the household is one-parent or two-parent are just two types of information collected. From the last census, we learned that most women work outside the home. That is a major change in American society. The census also told us the population is getting older and whether older people live alone. The growing population presents a challenge for the future. A smaller, younger population of wage earners will support a larger, older, population.

Our population is also more diverse. More and more Americans have a mixed heritage. Previously the census forms had few choices for people to identify their race or ethnic background. The twenty-first century census forms increased the categories from which people could choose.

List two things that we learned about the U.S. population in the last census.

A POPULATION ON THE MOVE

At the founding of the United States, most people lived on farms. The **migration** of the 1800s brought people to cities to take factory jobs. By the 1920s, more people lived in cities than in rural areas.

The invention of the car and the building of highways after World War II increased this trend. People no longer had to live near where they worked. Today more than 80 percent of the American people live in regions made up of cities and their suburbs.

Today, where does more than 80 percent of the U.S. population live?

CHALLENGE ACTIVITY

Critical Thinking: Explaining Write a paragraph explaining how a population of a nation can grow.

Original content © Houghton Mifflin Harcourt Publishing Company. Additions and changes to the original content are the responsibility of the instructor.

8 Guided Reading Workbook

The key terms from your textbook have been boldfaced, allowing you to quickly find and study them.

The challenge activity provides an opportunity for you to apply important critical thinking skills using the content that you learned in the section.

As you read each summary, be sure to complete the questions and activities in the margin boxes. They help you check your reading comprehension and track important content.

The third page of each section allows you to demonstrate your understanding of the key terms introduced in the section.

Some pages have a word bank. You can use it to help find answers or complete writing activities.

Writing activities require you to include key terms in what you write. Remember to check to make sure that you are using the terms correctly.

Various activities help you check your knowledge of key terms.

Name ______________ Class ______________ Date ______________

Section 3, *continued*

census	demographics	birthrate
death rate	migration	

DIRECTIONS Use the five vocabulary words from the word list to write a summary of what you learned in the section.

____

____

____

____

____

____

____

DIRECTIONS Read each sentence and fill in the blank with the word in the word pair that best completes the sentence.

1. The United States takes a ______________ every ten years. (census/demographic)
2. In the 1800s the ______________ of people to the cities changed the way of life in the United States. (birthrate/migration)
3. The ______________ of the population in the 1920s showed that many people had moved to the cities. (death rate/demographics)
4. In early America, the ______________ increased as many people had large families. (birthrate/death rate)
5. In its first century, the population increased as the United States gained new ______________. (territories/demographics)

Name ______________ Class ______________ Date ______________

We the People

Section 1

MAIN IDEA

As a U.S. citizen, it is your duty to help preserve freedom and to ensure justice and equality for yourself and all Americans.

Key Terms

civics the study of what it means to be a citizen

citizen a legally recognized member of a country

government the organizations, institutions, and individuals who exercise political authority over a group of people

Academic Vocabulary

values ideas that people hold dear and try to live by

Section Summary

WHY STUDY CIVICS?

The study of what it means to be a citizen in our country is called **civics**. In civics, we learn about our rights and responsibilities as **citizens**. The idea of the citizen started in Greece about 590 B.C. and then was later adopted by the Romans.

What it means to be a citizen has changed since the days of the Roman Republic. Today citizens have rights and responsibilities that differ from nation to nation. It depends on the type of **government** that runs each country.

Being a U.S. citizen means being an active and productive member of society. It means fulfilling your duties as a member of your family, school, and community.

Why do we study civics?

____

____

What do the rights and duties of citizens in different countries depend on?

____

____

____

AMERICAN VALUES

The U.S. Constitution and our laws give all Americans the same rights and freedoms. These are based on the American <u>values</u> of equality, liberty, and justice for all people.

Equality means that every citizen has the same rights and benefits. No one has more rights than any other citizen. Everyone is equal. All people in all groups have the same rights and benefits.

Underline the sentences that explain what *equality* is.

The creators of our government gave us a system that guarantees our liberty. Not everyone in the world has the basic freedoms we have. We can speak or write things without punishment. We are free to live and travel anywhere. We can get an education and take a job we want and practice religion.

Our legal system guarantees us justice. The government cannot send anyone to jail without proving, in a trial, that the law was broken.

QUALITIES OF A GOOD CITIZEN

With these guaranteed rights and freedoms come civic duties. We must follow the laws of our community, state, and country. We need to be willing to protect these freedoms and rights that, over the years, people have fought and died for.

What do good citizens need to tell their elected officials?

____

____

____

Voting is a very important duty for all citizens age 18 and older. In the United States, we govern ourselves through the officials we elect. If the elected officials do not respond to the voters, we can vote them out of office. Citizens also have the duty to tell officials if they agree or disagree with government actions.

More ways you can be a good citizen include believing in equal opportunity for all, respecting the opinions of others, and being loyal to and proud of our country.

CHALLENGE ACTIVITY

Critical Thinking: Explaining Write a diary entry that explains how you can be a good citizen in your school, community, state, and country.

DIRECTIONS Match the definition with the correct term from the right column.

_____ 1. ideas that people hold dear and try to live by

_____ 2. a legally recognized member of a country

_____ 3. the study of what it means to be a citizen

_____ 4. the organizations, institutions, and individuals who exercise political authority over a group of people

a. civics

b. citizen

c. government

d. values

DIRECTIONS Read each sentence and fill in the blank with the word that best completes the sentence.

5. As a U.S. citizen you have the duty to be a/an ____________________ and productive member of society. (active/passive)

6. Equality, liberty, and justice for all people are U.S. ____________________. (decrees/values)

7. The ____________________ guarantees citizens in the U.S. equality, liberty, and justice. (Constitution/Articles of Confederation)

8. To be a good citizen we need to follow the laws of our school, community, state and ____________________. (tribe/country)

9. ____________________ is a very important duty for all citizens age 18 and older. (Voting/Exercising)

10. The legal system in the U.S. guarantees people ____________________. (wealth/justice)

Section 2

MAIN IDEA

Throughout history, immigrants have brought their languages, ideas, beliefs, hopes, and customs to the United States. Their ways of life are constantly mixing with and influencing the culture of Americans who came before.

Key Terms

immigrants people who came from other countries

quota a system that allows into the United States each year just a specific number of immigrants from certain regions

aliens permanent residents of the U.S. who are citizens of another country

native-born people born in the United States

naturalization the legal process by which an alien may become a citizen

refugees people who are trying to escape dangers in their home countries

Section Summary

AMERICANS ARE FROM EVERYWHERE

People from various parts of the world have settled in the United States. They are called **immigrants**. They have brought their different languages, ideas, beliefs, customs, hopes, and dreams.

From what continent did the first Americans come?

____

____

____

In the past, the United States has been called a "melting pot" of various heritages. That means people came to the United States from all over and mostly adopted American customs.

Because many immigrants continue to practice their customs and traditions, some say it is more accurate to describe America as a salad bowl. In a salad, foods retain their individual, unique flavors.

Many scientists believe that the ancestors of American Indians came to North America from Asia between 12,000 and 40,000 years ago. Europeans eventually arrived to claim land and build settlements.

The news that America had vast natural resources spread through Europe. Soon, Europeans settled in the Caribbean, Mexico, Central and South America, and along the Atlantic coast of North America.

Africans also came to the Americas. They had been cruelly captured and enslaved. Many generations of Africans were forced to live in bondage in European colonies.

IMMIGRATION POLICY

After the American Revolution, the newly independent United States was founded on beliefs in human equality and basic freedoms. Even more people immigrated to the United States seeking freedom and jobs. By the mid-1800s thousands from Eastern Europe and China had settled here.

Why did more immigrants come to the United States after the American Revolution?

____

____

____

Businesses welcomed the newcomers. Some American laborers resented the immigrants because they worked for low wages. In the 1880s, Congress passed laws limiting immigration. In the 1920s, it passed laws that set a yearly **quota** for immigrants.

BECOMING A U.S. CITIZEN

Millions of immigrants have become U.S. citizens. All citizens have the same rights and responsibilities. Most citizens are **native-born**. Other people, called **aliens**, live here but are citizens of another country. Legal aliens have permission of the United States to live here. They cannot vote or hold public office. They must carry an I.D. card called a green card. Aliens can become citizens through the **naturalization** process.

Underline the sentence that means most U.S. citizens are born in the United States.

People who enter the United States illegally are called illegal aliens, or undocumented residents. People who come to the United States escaping danger in their home countries are called **refugees**. Each year the government sets a quota for refugees.

CHALLENGE ACTIVITY

Critical Thinking: Summarizing In an essay summarize the different ways people can become citizens of the United States.

aliens	quota	immigrants
native-born	refugees	naturalization

DIRECTIONS Answer each question by writing a sentence that contains at least one word from the word bank.

1. What are people called who moved to the United States from another country because of danger in their homeland?

2. What are permanent residents of the United States who are still citizens of another country called?

3. What did the immigration laws Congress passed in the 1920s set?

4. Most U.S. citizens are born in the United States and therefore called what?

5. What are people called who move from their homeland to another country?

6. How can aliens become citizens of the United States?

Name ______________________ Class ______________ Date ______________

We the People

Section 3

MAIN IDEA

The U.S. population continues to grow and change today.

Key Terms and People

census official periodic counting of a population

demographics the study of the characteristics or traits of a human population

birthrate the annual number of live births for every 1,000

death rate the annual number of deaths for every 1,000 members of the population

migration the movement of large numbers of people from region to region

Section Summary

THE CENSUS

The United States takes a **census** every ten years. Census information is used mainly to find out how many people live in each state. That determines how many representatives each state sends to the Congress. The census also shows if the population is growing or shrinking. The population of the United States is expected to grow by 50 million people by 2025.

How often does the United States take a census?

____

____

POPULATION GROWTH

The census reflects the **birthrate** and **death rate** of the people. The population of a country, however, grows in three ways. The birthrate among the population increases. A country adds new territory and its people. People immigrate to the country.

In early America, the birthrate increased as people had many children. Most people lived on farms and children helped the family work.

The United States expanded and gained new territories in its first century. That also increased the population, as the people living in those areas became citizens.

The immigration of people from other countries also added to the population. Since 1820, more than 60 million people have come to the United States.

POPULATION CHANGES

Information collected in the census tells us the **demographics** of the U.S. population. Lifestyles change, and the census shows us those changes. The number of people in each household and whether the household is one-parent or two-parent are just two types of information collected. From the last census, we learned that most women work outside the home. That is a major change in American society. The census also told us the population is getting older and whether older people live alone. The growing population presents a challenge for the future. A smaller, younger population of wage earners will support a larger, older, population.

List two things that we learned about the U.S. population in the last census.

____
____
____
____

Our population is also more diverse. More and more Americans have a mixed heritage. Previously the census forms had few choices for people to identify their race or ethnic background. The twenty-first century census forms increased the categories from which people could choose.

A POPULATION ON THE MOVE

At the founding of the United States, most people lived on farms. The **migration** of the 1800s brought people to cities to take factory jobs. By the 1920s, more people lived in cities than in rural areas.

The invention of the car and the building of highways after World War II increased this trend. People no longer had to live near where they worked. Today more than 80 percent of the American people live in regions made up of cities and their suburbs.

Today, where does more than 80 percent of the U.S. population live?

____
____
____
____

CHALLENGE ACTIVITY

Critical Thinking: Explaining Write a paragraph explaining how a population of a nation can grow.

census	demographics	birthrate
death rate	migration	

DIRECTIONS Use the five vocabulary words from the word list to write a summary of what you learned in the section.

____

____

____

____

____

____

____

____

DIRECTIONS Read each sentence and fill in the blank with the word in the word pair that best completes the sentence.

1. The United States takes a ______________________ every ten years. (census/demographic)

2. In the 1800s the ______________________ of people to the cities changed the way of life in the United States. (birthrate/migration)

3. The ______________________ of the population in the 1920s showed that many people had moved to the cities. (death rate/demographics)

4. In early America, the ______________________ increased as many people had large families. (birthrate/death rate)

5. In its first century, the population increased as the United States gained new ______________________. (territories/demographics)

Name ______________________ Class ______________ Date ______________

Foundations of Government

Section 1

MAIN IDEA

Government plays an essential role in every country. A country's government affects the lives of its people. Often, it affects people around the world.

Key Terms

monarch person who reigns over a kingdom or an empire

dictator person who rules with complete and absolute power

democracy government in which the people of a nation either rule directly or elect officials who act on their behalf

direct democracy government in which all voters meet in one place to make laws and decide what actions to take

representative democracy government in which people elect representatives to carry on the work of government for them

republic system of government in which people consent to be ruled by their elected leaders

constitution written plan of government

Academic Vocabulary

traditional customary, time-honored

Section Summary

TYPES OF GOVERNMENTS

Every country in the world has a government. These governments can be very different from one another. Each country's government has been shaped by the traditional beliefs of its people. There are two main government types: non-democratic and democratic.

What are the two main types of governments?

____

____

Citizens do not have ruling power in non-democratic governments. These governments include monarchies, dictatorships, and theocracies. A **monarch** is a person who reigns over a kingdom. A **dictator** is a person who rules with complete and absolute power. Theocracies are governments controlled by one or more religious leaders.

Underline three examples of non-democratic governments.

In a democratic government, or **democracy,** the people have the power to rule. A **direct democracy** is a government in which all voters meet to make government decisions. People in a **representative democracy** elect representatives to run the government for them. When people let elected leaders rule for them, it is called a **republic.** The United States is a republic.

In which type of democracy do voters meet to make government decisions?

____

____

PURPOSES OF GOVERNMENT

People in the United States have set up governments for a number of purposes. One is to allow people to live together in groups. Government helps people to solve problems and make life better for all.

Another purpose of government is to provide services. Governments often offer services that are very important or expensive. For instance, the federal government protects our nation from attacks. Other governments provide schools, highways, and police and fire protection.

The basic plan of American government is given in a **constitution.** This is a written plan of government. Under this plan, the government makes laws that people must know and obey.

What gives the basic plan of American government?

____

____

GUARANTEEING FREEDOM

American government has one additional purpose. This is to protect the rights and freedoms of all citizens. The nation's laws give citizens many freedoms, such as freedom of speech and freedom of religion. These laws also say that all citizens have equal rights.

Circle one type of freedom that the nation's laws give to citizens.

CHALLENGE ACTIVITY

Critical Thinking: Elaborating Review the list of services that government provides to citizens. Think of another service that government provides. Write a description of how this service affects your life.

DIRECTIONS On the line provided before each statement, write **T** if a statement is true or **F** if a statement is false. If the statement is false, find a word or phrase in the vocabulary list that makes the statement true. Write a new sentence on the line provided.

_____ 1. A monarch is a person who reigns over a kingdom or empire.

____

_____ 2. A dictator shares some ruling power with the people.

____

_____ 3. People have the power to rule in a democracy.

____

_____ 4. Voters meet to make government decisions in a direct democracy.

____

_____ 5. Citizens do not hold elections in a representative democracy.

____

_____ 6. Citizens do not allow others to have ruling authority in a republic.

____

_____ 7. The basic plan for American government is given in a constitution.

____

_____ 8. A people's traditional beliefs are those that are customary and time-honored.

____

Name ______________________ Class ______________ Date ______________

Foundations of Government

Section 2

MAIN IDEA

The American ideals that people should rule themselves and that government should protect human rights are clearly set forth in the Declaration of Independence.

Key Terms

human rights basic rights to which all people are entitled

confederation a loose association, rather than a firm union, of states

sovereignty absolute power

Section Summary

THE DECLARATION OF INDEPENDENCE

The American colonies went to war against Great Britain in 1775. Colonists were angry about new taxes and other steps taken by the British Parliament. In 1776, a group called the Continental Congress met in Philadelphia. Their goal was to write a Declaration of Independence. Thomas Jefferson wrote most of the Declaration of Independence. The Continental Congress approved this document on July 4, 1776.

What was the purpose of the Declaration of Independence?

____

____

The Declaration of Independence explains why the colonies wanted to form their own separate nation. The colonists thought the power of the government should come from the people. They said that if a government ignores what its people want, the people have a right to change the government.

Because of these ideas, the Declaration of Independence has become a statement of American ideals. It says that government should protect **human rights.** These are the basic rights to which all people are entitled. Today, the words of the Declaration of Independence mean that all Americans are equal under the law. It has become one of the greatest documents in American history.

Why has the Declaration of Independence become an important document in American history?

____

____

THE ARTICLES OF CONFEDERATION

The Declaration of Independence contained many important ideas. However, it was not a plan of government for the new nation. In 1777, the Continental Congress adopted a plan of government called the Articles of Confederation. This new government took effect in 1781. After the Revolutionary War, the colonies became a confederation called the United States of America. A **confederation** is a loose association, rather than a firm union, of states.

Under this government, the states shared equal powers. The national government was a lawmaking body called Congress. It had very limited powers. Most people still feared a strong national government like that of Great Britain. The writers of the Articles of Confederation wanted to protect states' **sovereignty,** or absolute power.

Underline the statement that describes the structure of the national government under the Articles of Confederation.

However, the new nation faced many problems. The Articles of Confederation did not give the national government the powers it needed to solve many of these problems. In 1787, Congress called for a meeting to discuss changing the Articles.

Did the state governments or national government have more power under the Articles of Confederation?

____

____

WEAKNESSES OF THE ARTICLES

The main weakness of the Articles of Confederation was the relationship between the state and national governments. States acted like small, separate nations. The national government did not have the power to enforce or interpret its laws. When states disobeyed these laws, tensions grew between the state and national governments.

What caused tensions to grow between the state and national governments?

____

____

CHALLENGE ACTIVITY

Critical Thinking: Evaluating Write a brief paragraph discussing how colonists' conflicts with Great Britain eventually led to a different type of problem with the new government they formed after gaining independence.

human rights	confederation	sovereignty

DIRECTIONS Answer each question by writing a sentence that contains at least one term from the word bank.

1. How did the writers of the Articles of Confederation address the powers of the states?

____

____

2. How did the government of the colonies change after the Revolutionary War ended?

____

____

3. What ideal did the Declaration of Independence present for American government?

____

____

MAIN IDEA

The framers of the U.S. Constitution drew upon a history of democratic ideals while developing a document that would establish a new, stronger federal government.

Key Terms

Parliament the lawmaking body of Great Britain

federalism a federal system of government

compromise an agreement in which each side gives up something in order to reach a solution

ratification approval

Federalists supporters of the Constitution who favored a strong national government

Antifederalists people who opposed the Constitution and the federal system of government

Section Summary

THE CONSTITUTIONAL CONVENTION AND HISTORY

In 1787, a group of delegates gathered to fix the Articles of Confederation. Instead, they wrote a completely new plan for our government. This plan became the Constitution.

The delegates at the Constitutional Convention were influenced by their British heritage. They took principles from the Magna Carta, the English Bill of Rights, and Britain's parliamentary government. **Parliament** is the lawmaking body of Great Britain.

Circle the British influences on the delegates to the Constitutional Convention.

These delegates held their meetings in secret. They wanted to discuss the government openly and avoid the input of outsiders. The framers of the Constitution knew they had to give the national government more power. They also wanted the states to keep the powers needed to govern themselves. To do this, the framers established **federalism.** This is a system in which the national government and state governments share power.

Why were the meetings of the convention held in secret?

____

____

The delegates disagreed on many issues as they wrote the Constitution. They often settled these disagreements through compromises. A **compromise** is an agreement in which each side gives up something in order to reach a solution.

GOVERNMENT BECOMES STRONGER

The new Constitution increased the strength of the national government. Congress gained new powers, and a president and Supreme Court were added to the national government.

The delegates had finished the Constitution by September 1787. Most of the delegates believed they had written the best plan for government possible. However, the Constitution still had to be sent to the states for **ratification,** or approval. To take effect, 9 of the 13 states had to ratify it. Many people began to debate whether the Constitution should be approved. **Federalists** were supporters of the Constitution. They favored a strong national government. **Antifederalists** opposed the new Constitution. They believed the federal system of government would not protect the rights of states or individuals.

How did the new Constitution affect the national government?

____

____

THE CONSTITUTION IS RATIFIED

The Federalists gained support over time. However, some citizens and states still believed that the Constitution should contain a list of the rights of people. The Constitution was ratified in 1788. The new government took effect in 1789.

What group of people would have wanted the Constitution to include a list of rights?

____

____

CHALLENGE ACTIVITY

Critical Thinking: Contrasting Identify how the viewpoints of the Federalists and Antifederalists differed. Design a graphic organizer that presents these differences clearly.

DIRECTIONS Match the terms in the first column with their correct definitions from the second column by placing the letter of the correct definition in the space provided before each term.

_____ 1. Parliament

_____ 2. federalism

_____ 3. compromise

_____ 4. ratification

_____ 5. Federalists

_____ 6. Antifederalists

a. supporters of the Constitution; favored a strong national government

b. a system in which the national government and state governments share power

c. opponents of the Constitution; believed it would not protect the rights of states and individuals

d. an agreement in which each side gives up something in order to reach a solution

e. the lawmaking body of Great Britain

f. approval

MAIN IDEA

The Constitution is an agreement between the citizens of the United States and the government. The Constitution states that the people will grant powers to the government. In return, the government is to carry out the goals of the Constitution.

Key Terms

popular sovereignty government by the consent of the governed

Preamble the introduction to the Constitution

limited government a government that has specific restrictions on its power

majority rule a principle that in a disagreement, everyone will accept the decision of the majority (most of the people)

delegated powers the powers that the Constitution specifically gives to the federal government

reserved powers the powers that are set aside for, or reserved for, the states because they are not specifically given to the federal government

concurrent powers the powers shared by both the federal government and state government

Academic Vocabulary

federal referring to the national government

Section Summary

PILGRIMS INFLUENCED THE FRAMERS

The Pilgrims created their own rules of government in the Mayflower Compact. They all agreed to obey these rules. Years later, this Compact influenced the Framers who wrote the Constitution.

Like the Compact, the Constitution would create a government whose power came from the "consent of the people." This is called **popular sovereignty**.

The **Preamble,** or introduction, to the Constitution begins with the words "We the people." These words show that the people agree to the powers they are giving to their government.

Who wrote the rules of the Mayflower Compact?

____

____

The words "We the people" are found in what part of the U.S. Constitution?

____

____

REACHING THE GOALS OF THE CONSTITUTION

The Framers had several goals in mind when writing the Constitution. One goal was **limited government**, or restrictions on government power. The Constitution also states that disagreements within the government should be settled by **majority rule** in which everyone accepts the decision of most of the people.

A few years after the Constitution became the law of the land, the people added the Bill of Rights to the Constitution. These amendments to the Constitution set out the rights of every citizen.

What does the Bill of Rights describe?

____

____

POWERS OF THE FEDERAL AND STATE GOVERNMENTS

The Framers of the Constitution did not want a central government that was too strong. They wanted power to be shared between the federal and state governments. This is called a federalist system, in which the federal, or national, government has limited powers and state governments have their own powers.

Delegated powers are powers the Constitution gives to the federal government in Washington, D.C. Delegated powers include the power to print money and maintain an army.

States exercise what are called **reserved powers**. These include the power to collect state taxes and to run local elections.

Concurrent powers are shared by both federal and state governments. Collecting taxes and making laws are concurrent powers. Both state and federal laws must follow the Constitution.

Which government has delegated powers from the Constitution, and which government has reserved powers?

____

____

CHALLENGE ACTIVITY

Critical Thinking: Applying Write a set of rules that might apply to governing your class, including the rights and responsibilities of teachers and students. Present your idea and hold a vote to see if it is approved by a majority.

DIRECTIONS Match the definition with the correct term from the right column.

_____ 1. A government with specific restrictions on its power.

_____ 2. The introduction to the Constitution.

_____ 3. These are the powers given by the Constitution to the federal government.

_____ 4. Government by the consent of the governed.

_____ 5. These are powers set aside for the states.

_____ 6. A principle that in a disagreement, everyone will accept the decision of most of the people.

_____ 7. These are powers that are shared by both the federal and the state government.

_____ 8. This is the term used to refer to the national government.

a. popular sovereignty
b. delegated powers
c. limited government
d. majority rule
e. concurrent powers
f. Preamble
g. reserved powers
h. federal

Name ______________ Class ______________ Date ______________

The United States Constitution

Section 2

MAIN IDEA

The Constitution prevents any person or part of the government from taking too much power. It does this by creating three separate branches in the federal government. The power of the federal government is distributed among the three branches.

Key Terms

separation of powers the separate powers that are divided among the three branches of the federal government

legislative branch the Congress, which makes laws and is the part of the federal government made up of elected representatives of the people of each state

executive branch the president, vice president, and the cabinet, as well as agency and department heads; the executive branch carries out laws

judicial branch the federal courts that interpret the meaning of the laws passed by Congress and determine if they follow the Constitution

checks and balances the system set up by the Framers to give each branch of the federal government the power to limit the actions, or power, of other branches

veto the power of the president to reject, or not sign, a law passed by Congress

judicial review the power of the courts to review the acts of other branches of government and decide if they have acted correctly and according to the Constitution

Section Summary

SEPARATION OF POWERS

The Framers were certain that any government that had too much power would become a "tyranny." They were determined not to give too much power to any one part of the government. So they created a federal government that had three parts. Each part would have its own distinct powers. This is called **separation of powers**. It makes sure that each branch of government has limited power.

How did the Framers prevent tyranny from arising in the government?

____

____

THE THREE BRANCHES OF GOVERNMENT

The **legislative branch** of the federal government is the Congress, which makes the laws. Congress also controls the way government spends money.

The **executive branch** of the federal government carries out, or executes, the laws passed by Congress. The president is the head of the executive branch. The vice president, heads of departments, and agencies are also part of the executive branch.

The **judicial branch** of government includes the federal courts, which interpret the meaning of the laws passed by Congress. The Supreme Court is the highest court in the land. It determines if laws follow the Constitution.

CHECKS AND BALANCES

Each branch of government has the ability to limit the power of the other two branches. This is the principle of **checks and balances**.

The president can check the power of Congress with a veto. A **veto** rejects a law when the president refuses to sign it. Congress can check the president by overriding the veto. If enough members of Congress vote for the law, the president's veto is rejected and the law passes. The judicial branch can check both the executive and legislative branches by reviewing the laws that are passed.

Who can use a veto to reject a law passed by Congress?

____

____

The judicial branch can strike down any law that does not follow the Constitution. **Judicial review** is the principle that gives the Supreme Court the power to determine if laws and acts of the president follow the Constitution.

CHALLENGE ACTIVITY

Critical Thinking: Flow Chart Draw a chart that shows how checks and balances may affect a law that is passed by Congress.

legislative branch	veto	judicial branch
checks and balances	executive branch	separation of powers
judicial review		

DIRECTIONS Read each sentence and fill in the blank with the term from the word bank that best completes the sentence.

1. The Framers created a ________________ by setting up three branches of government, with each having its own unique role.

2. The president can use a ________________ to reject a law passed by Congress.

3. The vice president is the second most powerful person in the ________________ of the federal government.

4. The Supreme Court has the power of ________________ to interpret laws and determine if they follow the Constitution.

5. Congress makes up the ________________ of the federal government, which makes laws.

6. The Constitution sets up a system of ________________ in which each branch of the federal government is able to limit the power of the other branches.

7. Federal courts are all part of the ________________ of the government.

Name ______________________ Class ______________ Date ______________

The United States Constitution

Section 3

MAIN IDEA

The Constitution is an enduring document. The Constitution has met the needs of a changing country for more than 200 years.

Key Terms

amendment a written change to the Constitution that has been approved by the people

repeal to cancel or do away with, as in a constitutional amendment

cabinet a group of the president's closest and most important advisers

Section Summary

ENVISIONING CHANGE

The Framers wrote the Constitution with the understanding that it would have to guide the nation for a long time. For more than 200 years, the Constitution has guided the country. Yet it has been altered as times and needs have changed. The Framers wrote into the Constitution a process the nation should follow to change the Constitution.

Circle how long the United States has had its Constitution.

CHANGING THE CONSTITUTION

A change made to the Constitution is called an **amendment**. The Framers wrote into the Constitution the steps in the amendment process. An amendment can be made in two ways. It can be proposed by a two-thirds vote in both houses of Congress. Or two-thirds of the state legislatures can ask Congress to hold a national convention to propose the amendment.

What is an amendment?

____

____

After the amendment is proposed, it must be ratified, or approved. Two-thirds of state legislatures may approve it. Or special state conventions may be held to approve it.

The Framers also wrote about the process of canceling an amendment, or how to **repeal** it. If people do not like the effects of an amendment, they can follow a process to repeal it. The repealed amendment is taken out of the Constitution.

The Constitution does not have lots of details about government. Instead, it sets broad guidelines for governing. This gives the government the flexibility it needs to adapt to new challenges. For example, George Washington, the first president, appointed his **cabinet**, a group of advisers who helped him. The cabinet is not mentioned in the Constitution. Yet it is one of many things that have become a tradition in government.

What does the cabinet do?

____

____

The Constitution does guide the laws that are passed by Congress. Often, before writing a law, members of Congress study the Constitution to make sure that the proposed law follows it. If there is any question about the law after it is passed, the Supreme Court may review the law. The Court decides if the law follows the Constitution.

CHALLENGE ACTIVITY

Critical Thinking: Assessing/Evaluating Do you think the Framers were correct in writing the Constitution using vague language? Why or why not? Explain your answer, using examples.

repeal	amendment	cabinet

DIRECTIONS Use at least one vocabulary word from the word bank to answer each of the following questions.

1. What is one way you might want to change the Constitution? Why do you think it needs this change? What would you do to get this change?

____

____

____

____

2. Is there any part of the Constitution that you think should be removed from the document? What part should be canceled? Why should it be canceled? Explain your reason for wanting to make this change to the Constitution.

____

____

____

____

3. The Constitution does not mention anything about allowing the president to have a group of advisers to help him make decisions. Do you think having advisers is against the Constitution? Should traditions, such as having advisers, be allowed even though they are not specifically permitted by the Constitution? Why or why not? Explain your reasons.

____

____

____

____

MAIN IDEA

The freedoms spelled out in the Bill of Rights—the freedoms of religion, speech, the press, and petition, and the right to a speedy and fair trial—are essential to our democratic system.

Key Terms

Bill of Rights the first ten amendments to the U.S. Constitution, focusing on individual rights

separation of church and state guarantees individuals the freedom to practice any religion—or none—and prevents the government from establishing an official religion that everybody in the country must practice

self-incrimination the Fifth Amendment guarantees that individuals cannot be forced to testify against themselves and also protects them from double jeopardy

due process of law requires that the government act in accordance with existing law when it deprives a citizen of her or his life, liberty, or property

eminent domain under the Fifth Amendment the government may take individuals' property, for the common good, in exchange for fair compensation

bail the Eighth Amendment prevents the courts from setting excessive bail in cases

Section Summary

ADDING THE BILL OF RIGHTS

When the Constitution was first ratified by the 13 states it did not include the **Bill of Rights**, or the list of specific individual rights and protections from the government. Some leaders argued that the people did not need a separate bill of rights. Others, including Thomas Jefferson, argued that a bill of rights would protect the people from the government. He remembered the way Britain treated its American colonists. By 1791 the states approved the first ten amendments—known as the Bill of Rights—to the Constitution.

According to Thomas Jefferson, what purpose would a bill of rights serve?

____

____

____

FIRST AMENDMENT PROTECTS PERSONAL FREEDOMS

The First Amendment deals with some of Americans' most basic freedoms. It allows individuals to practice any religion—or none. It requires the government to maintain a **separation of church and state**. Individuals and the media can speak freely without punishment. People can assemble, or gather together. The First Amendment also protects Americans' right to contact government leaders with their grievances.

List three key freedoms guaranteed by the First Amendment:

____

____

____

OTHER RIGHTS GUARANTEED BY THE BILL OF RIGHTS

The Second and Third Amendments protect citizens' right to bear arms and to not have soldiers quartered in their homes. The Fourth Amendment prohibits unlawful searches by the police. The Fifth Amendment bars the government from forcing individuals to provide evidence against themselves, or **self-incrimination**. It also forces the government to follow **due process of law** by investigating, trying, and punishing individuals only in ways allowed by law. The Fifth Amendment's **eminent domain** clause allows the government to take property for public use, but in exchange for fair compensation. The Sixth Amendment ensures the rights to a jury trial and legal representation. The Seventh Amendment protects the rights of those accused of some financial or property crimes. The Eighth Amendment prohibits cruel and unusual punishment. It also allows people to apply for release on **bail** before their trial.

Which amendments protect citizens who are accused of crimes?

____

____

____

____

CHALLENGE ACTIVITY

Critical Thinking: Making Inferences The U.S. Constitution was adopted after the colonies gained their independence. What experiences might have made leaders such as Thomas Jefferson think that a bill of rights should be added to the Constitution?

Bill of Rights	self-incrimination	eminent domain
separation of church and state	due process of law	bail

DIRECTIONS On the line provided before each statement, write **T** if a statement is true or **F** if a statement is false. If the statement is false, find a word or phrase in the word bank that makes the statement true. Write a new sentence on the line provided.

_____ 1. Eminent domain happens when someone accused of a crime is forced to provide evidence against herself or himself.

____

_____ 2. Due process of law requires the government to fairly compensate citizens whose property they take for public use.

____

_____ 3. Bail is money paid by people accused of a crime so that they can be freed from jail before and during their trial.

____

_____ 4. The Bill of Rights is the first 10 amendments to the Constitution.

____

_____ 5. Separation of church and state identifies citizens' rights and the ways they are protected from the government.

____

_____ 6. Self-incrimination means the government must deal with an individual accused of a crime only in ways allowed by law.

____

MAIN IDEA

Other amendments to the Constitution expanded the civil rights of Americans.

Key Terms

civil rights rights guaranteed to all U.S. citizens

suffrage the right to vote

poll tax a tax people must pay to register to vote

Academic Vocabulary

principles basic beliefs, rules, or laws

Section Summary

AMENDMENTS EXTEND CIVIL RIGHTS

Although the Bill of Rights did much to protect individuals' **civil rights**, it did not spell out what all of those rights were. This left the states with the job of defining and safeguarding some important freedoms. However, these freedoms did not always apply to all citizens. Worse, some states took advantage of the opportunity to deny large groups of people their basic rights. They kept some groups from becoming citizens and denied others the right to vote. Finally, the Civil War led to new constitutional amendments that provided more freedoms to more people.

Although President Abraham Lincoln's Emancipation Proclamation outlawed slavery, it applied only to the Confederate States. Thus, it could not be enforced until the Union won the war. The Thirteenth Amendment, ratified after the war, outlawed slavery throughout the United States. In 1868, the Fourteenth Amendment gave the right of citizenship to African Americans. It also required

Why did Lincoln's Emancipation Proclamation not free all enslaved people?

____

____

____

____

____

____

____

states to protect citizens' rights to due process and equal protection under the law.

AMENDMENTS EXTEND VOTING RIGHTS

Our founders valued participation in government, viewing it as one of the key principles of a democracy. However, they did not create a society in which all citizens could participate by voting. Between 1870 and 1971, six amendments to the U.S. Constitution extended the **suffrage**, or right to vote. The Fifteenth Amendment, ratified in 1870, made it illegal to restrict voting rights because of color or race. In 1913, the Seventeenth Amendment allowed voters to elect senators directly. Before then, state legislators elected senators who would represent their states.

Despite these changes, women still could not vote in national elections. Although some states had gradually begun giving women the right to vote, no law required every state to do so. In 1920, the Nineteenth Amendment extended suffrage to women throughout the country. Residents of Washington, D.C. did not win the right to vote in presidential elections until ratification of the Twenty-Third Amendment in 1961. The **poll tax** charged in some states as a fee for voter registration made voting impossible for many Americans who could not afford to vote. The Twenty-Fourth Amendment prohibited these taxes in national elections. In 1971, the Twenty-Sixth Amendment lowered the voting age from 21 to 18 years. This amendment ensured that people who could be drafted into military service had the right to vote.

Which amendments extended voting rights to women and to people 18 years of age?

____

____

____

____

CHALLENGE ACTIVITY

Critical Thinking: Analyzing Some former slave states charged poll taxes after the Fifteenth Amendment was passed. What does this suggest about which Americans were targeted by poll taxes?

civil rights	suffrage	poll tax
principles		

DIRECTIONS Read each sentence and fill in the blank with the term in the word pair that best completes the sentence.

1. The right to vote is known as _____________________________. (civil rights/suffrage)
2. The _____________________________ tended to keep many Americans from voting. (poll tax/principles)
3. Right or rights guaranteed to all citizens is/are _____________________________. (suffrage/civil rights)
4. Basic beliefs, rules, or laws are _____________________________. (principles/civil rights)

DIRECTIONS Use the four vocabulary words from the word bank to write a summary of what you learned in the section.

____

____

____

____

____

____

____

____

____

____

Name ______________________ Class ______________ Date ______________

Rights and Responsibilities

Section 3

MAIN IDEA

Along with the rights and freedoms of U.S. citizenship come important duties and responsibilities.

Key Terms

draft a law that requires men of a certain age to serve in the military

rationed in wartime the use of certain goods, foods, and resources by individuals may be limited so that more are available for the military

jury duty citizens may be called upon to serve on a jury during a trial

Section Summary

DUTIES OF CITIZENSHIP

Citizens must always be aware of their rights and understand their duties. One of the most basic duties is to obey the law. Because we must understand the law and other important matters, all citizens have a duty to be educated.

Citizens have a duty to pay taxes. Taxes provide money that the government uses to offer needed services. Courts, schools, and the military are examples of government services. Some citizens consider it their duty to serve in the military. The law makes it the duty of men between the ages of 18 and 25 to register for the **draft**. The government may call upon some of them to serve in times of war. Other citizens help during wartime by volunteering to send care packages to soldiers. They also avoid using too many goods that are restricted in supply, or **rationed**.

Some duties that citizens perform help protect the rights of other citizens. An individual has the right to a fair trial before a jury of his or her peers. This means that other citizens have the duty to appear in court if called upon. There they may serve as witnesses, or they may perform **jury duty**.

What duties do citizens perform to help protect the rights of other citizens?

____

____

RESPONSIBILITIES OF CITIZENSHIP

Citizens also have responsibilities. These are things that the law does not make them do. However, meeting these responsibilities makes them better citizens. Voting is an important responsibility. It helps make sure we have good leaders. It is also a way for citizens to let their leaders know how they feel about political issues. To do these things, citizens must be aware of important events and issues. This means that citizens also have a responsibility to be informed.

Citizens have the responsibility to take part in government. We might do this by participating in political campaigns or even by running for office. Educating others about important issues is another way of participating. Citizens do not have to wait for leaders to make changes. By participating in government, citizens can ask for changes needed.

What are three responsibilities that citizens have?

____

____

____

Helping others is another responsibility. There are many ways we can help in our own communities. Volunteering is a way to use our knowledge and skills to help others. By working to make others' lives better we also improve our community.

We also help others by respecting their rights. Being aware of our own rights makes it easier to respect the rights of others. It also helps us to speak out when an individual's rights are violated. In this way the government can take action by enforcing the law or by passing new laws.

CHALLENGE ACTIVITY

Critical Thinking: Writing to Explore Imagine that you are organizing volunteers in your community. What are some ways you believe they could help make your community a better place to live?

draft	rationed	jury duty

DIRECTIONS Answer each question by writing a sentence that contains at least one term from the word bank.

1. What is a way that the government is able to restrict the use of goods, foods, or resources that are needed by the military during wartime?

____

____

2. What duty does the law require citizens to perform in court other than serving as a witness?

____

____

3. While many citizens volunteer to serve in the military during times of peace and in war, under what kind of law are some citizens required to serve?

____

____

DIRECTIONS Use the three vocabulary terms from the word bank to write a summary of what you learned in the section.

____

____

____

____

____

____

Name ____________ Class ____________ Date ____________

The Legislative Branch

Section 1

MAIN IDEA

Congress is divided into two houses, the Senate and the House of Representatives, and its members have certain qualifications.

Key Terms

bicameral legislature a lawmaking body of two houses

apportioned distributed

gerrymandering practice of drawing district lines that favor a particular political party, politician, or group of people

immunity legal protection

expulsion state of having to give up one's seat in Congress

censure formal disapproval of a member's actions

Section Summary

TWO HOUSES OF CONGRESS

The legislative branch of the national or federal government, or Congress, makes laws for the country. Congress is made up of two houses—the House of Representatives and the Senate. This **bicameral legislature** guarantees that large and small states are represented fairly and assures that each house can check the actions of the other.

On a separate sheet of paper, draw a diagram that shows the two houses of Congress. Under each house, write its characteristics.

There are 435 members in the House of Representatives. The number of members **apportioned** to each state is based on the state's population as determined by the census. Each state is guaranteed at least one representative. In addition, Washington, D.C.; Guam; American Samoa; and the Virgin Islands each send one non-voting delegate to the House. States are divided into districts, and voters in each district elect a representative. District boundaries are based on population and **gerrymandering.** Elections are held in even-numbered years, and representatives are elected for two-year terms. If a representative dies or resigns before the end of his or her term, the state governor calls for a special election.

There are 100 members in the Senate—two from each state. Elections for one-third of Senators are held in even-numbered years for six-year terms. If a senator dies or resigns before the end of his or her term, the state governor may appoint a substitute until the next election. There are no term limits for the members of Congress.

MEMBERS OF CONGRESS

To be elected to the House of Representatives, a candidate must meet these requirements: be 25 years of age, be a U.S. citizen for seven years, and be a legal resident of the state of representation. To be elected to the Senate, a candidate must meet these requirements: be 30 years of age, be a U.S. citizen for nine years, and be a legal resident of the state of representation.

Why do you think there are requirements to be elected to Congress?

____

____

____

In exchange for service, the members of Congress earn yearly salaries. They also receive these benefits: local and federal offices, money to pay for staffs and office supplies, free trips home, free postage, and legal **immunity** while working.

Because the members of Congress are paid government workers, they must follow codes of conduct to show that they are honest. For example, there are limits on outside income, and members must make their finances public. If a member of Congress does meet this required code of conduct, he or she may be subject to **expulsion** or **censure.**

Do you agree or disagree that the members of Congress should not have term limits? Explain.

____

____

____

CHALLENGE ACTIVITY

Critical Thinking: Apply You have been asked to nominate someone you know to run for Congress. Write a Letter to the Editor of a local newspaper in which you nominate this person and explain his or her qualifications for the House or Senate.

DIRECTIONS For each item, provide an answer and an example or explanation.

1. Does a bicameral legislature have one, two, or three houses?

____

____

2. Which government action defines how seats in the House of Representatives are apportioned—an election or the census?

____

____

3. Would a congressional district created through gerrymandering have straight or oddly shaped boundary lines?

____

____

4. Which member of Congress might need immunity—one who is about to be arrested or one who has a contagious disease?

____

____

5. Which member of Congress might be subject to expulsion—one who accepts bribes or one who does not work enough?

____

____

6. Which member of Congress might be subject to censure—one who speaks too much or one who neglects to pay taxes?

____

____

MAIN IDEA

Congress is organized in a way that allows its members to pass legislation without each member having to do everything.

Key Terms

sessions congressional meeting periods, one for each year of a two-year term

caucuses private party meetings

president pro tempore Senate member elected to preside over the daily meetings of the Senate in place of the vice president

whip assistant to a party's floor leader

Speaker of the House leader who presides over House sessions

Section Summary

TERMS AND SESSIONS

A term of Congress begins at noon on January 3 of every odd-numbered year. However, Congress may change this date if necessary. Thus, a term lasts for two years. Congress must meet once during each of the two years of a term. Therefore, each term is divided into two **sessions,** one for each year of a term. When the work of a session is complete, both houses of Congress adjourn and the session ends. In a unique case, the president has the power to call Congress back into a special session after it has ended. Generally, the House and Senate members meet independently. However, sometimes they meet together in a joint session.

Underline the phrase that explains when both houses of Congress adjourn.

ORGANIZATION OF CONGRESS

At the beginning of each term, Republicans and Democrats meet in **caucuses** to choose their leaders. Voters elect members of Congress. The party with the most members is known as the majority party. The party with the fewest members is known as the minority party.

Who chooses the majority party?

____

____

According to the Constitution, the vice president of the United States is the president of the Senate. However, for day-to-day business, the majority party elects a **president pro tempore** to preside in the vice president's absence. Each party chooses a Senate floor leader, known as the majority leader and the minority leader. Each leader has an assistant known as a **whip.** The whip counts votes, encourages party loyalty, and maintains party attendance for important votes.

When a bill or a proposed law comes to the Senate, it is assigned to one of about twenty committees for review. Each committee is divided into subcommittees that study bills on behalf of the committee. Each committee and subcommittee is headed by a majority chairperson and a high-ranking minority member.

Suppose that you have introduced legislation to protect the Florida Everglades. On a separate sheet of paper, create a diagram to show how the Senate might study this bill.

The **Speaker of the House,** a member of the majority party, presides over the House of Representatives. The Speaker decides the order of business for the House and calls on members to speak. Like the Senate, the House uses committees and subcommittees to study bills.

Underline the tasks of the Speaker of the House.

CHALLENGE ACTIVITY

Critical Thinking: Comparing Use a Venn diagram to compare and contrast the organization of the Senate with the House of Representatives. Remember to place similarities where the circles overlap and differences in the outer circles. Based on your analysis, are the two houses more alike or more different?

DIRECTIONS Place terms from the word bank into the diagram where appropriate. You may use some terms more than one time.

sessions	caucuses	president pro tempore
whips	Speaker of the House	

U.S. Congress

Term beginning on January 3 will be made up of two **1.** ____________.

Senate	**House of Representatives**
President of the Senate or **2.** ________	**3.** ________________
Majority and Minority Leaders	Majority and Minority Leaders
Majority and Minority **4.** ________	Majority and Minority **5.** ________
Party Leadership elected by **6.** ________	Party Leadership elected by **7.** ________
Committees	Committees
Subcommittees	Subcommittees

DIRECTIONS Using terms from the word bank, discuss whether the organization of the U.S. Congress is effective.

____

____

____

____

____

____

____

____

____

MAIN IDEA

The Constitution both defines and limits the powers of Congress.

Key Terms

implied powers congressional powers to do any actions relating to delegated powers that are considered "necessary and proper"

elastic clause another name for the "necessary and proper" clause

impeach to accuse an officeholder of misconduct

treason an act that betrays or endangers one's country

Section Summary

CONGRESSIONAL POWERS

The Constitution assigns powers to Congress in five areas: government finance, trade and industry, defense, the court system, and growth. To pay government expenses, Congress may raise and collect taxes and borrow and print money. To defend the country and its laws, Congress may declare war, maintain an army, and create national courts. Congress may pass laws that control trade and immigration. It can also govern U.S. territories.

Underline the stated powers of Congress.

In addition to the stated powers of Congress, the Constitution suggests that Congress has other powers, as well. The Constitution states that Congress has the power to make all laws that are "necessary and proper" for it to carry out its stated powers. These **implied powers** are sometimes referred to as the **elastic clause** of the Constitution because they allow Congress to stretch or flex its powers.

Draw a box around the implied powers of Congress.

Congress also has the power to **impeach** government officials, or bring individuals accused of crimes or bad behavior to trial. If an official is found guilty of a serious crime such as **treason,** Congress may remove this person from office. The

What is the difference between a stated power of Congress and an implied power?

____

____

____

process of accusing and charging an official is the responsibility of the House of Representatives. The process of trying an official is the responsibility of the Senate.

The Constitution gives each house of Congress special powers. The House of Representatives starts all bills related to raising money, has the power to impeach officials, and chooses the president when no candidate receives enough electoral votes to be elected. The Senate has four special powers. It holds impeachment trials, chooses the vice president when no candidate receives enough electoral votes to be elected, approves treaties with foreign nations, and approves high officials appointed by the president.

Why are special powers divided between the House and the Senate?

____

____

____

LIMITS ON POWERS

While the Constitution gives some powers to Congress, it also limits the powers of Congress. For example, based on the Tenth Amendment, state governments, not Congress, have the power to run elections, manage schools, and create marriage laws. In addition, Congress does *not* have any of the following powers: apply new laws to past deeds, sentence people without trials, cancel court orders, tax exports, create laws that go against the Bill of Rights, show trade favoritism toward a state, grant royal or noble titles, or withdraw money without the support of a law.

Why might the Constitution guarantee some powers to state governments?

____

____

____

CHALLENGE ACTIVITY

Critical Thinking: Analyzing In a short essay, explain how power is balanced between the House of Representatives, the Senate, the president, the courts, and state governments. Make sure to provide specific examples in your explanation. Conclude by stating why this balance of power is an important part of the U.S. government.

DIRECTIONS Explain the relationship between each pair of words or terms.

1. implied powers : elastic clause

____

____

____

____

____

____

____

____

____

____

2. impeach : treason

____

____

____

____

____

____

____

____

____

____

Name ______________________ Class ______________ Date ______________

The Legislative Branch

Section 4

MAIN IDEA

To become a law, a bill goes through a multistage process involving both houses of Congress.

Key Terms

bill a proposed law

appropriation bill a bill approving the spending of money

act a law

filibuster a Senate discussion method intended to delay the vote on a bill

cloture a legislative procedure for ending debate in the Senate and taking a vote

veto a presidential rejection of a bill

pocket veto a ten-day delay in the presidential signing of a bill while Congress is not in session with the effect of killing the bill

Academic Vocabulary

procedure a series of steps by which a task is completed

Section Summary

HOW A BILL BEGINS

A **bill** or proposed law may begin in either house of Congress. It must be passed by both houses and signed by the president to become a law or **act.** There is one exception to this process. An **appropriation bill,** or a bill approving spending money, must begin in the House of Representatives.

Underline how a bill becomes a law.

THE HOUSE AND THE SENATE CONSIDER THE BILL

After a representative or senator introduces a bill, it is labeled. Then, the bill is printed in the *Congressional Record,* a document of the daily happenings in Congress.

Next, the bill is assigned to a regular congressional committee. This committee may send the bill to a subcommittee for review or kill the bill by setting it aside. If the bill survives, the committee holds hearings in which people testify

List two options a committee has for a bill.

1. ______________________

____

2. ______________________

____

Why do you think committees hear from people in favor of and against a bill?

for or against the bill. After a hearing, the committee may pass the bill, change and then pass the bill, or vote to kill it.

When a House committee passes a bill, it is returned to the House of Representatives for consideration. Here, members may debate and amend the bill. If a majority of House members vote to pass a bill, it is sent to the Senate.

Bills introduced in the Senate or passed by the House undergo the same process in the Senate. They are sent to committee and then back to the Senate for a vote. While the Speaker of the House has the power to limit debate in the House, Senators are not limited unless three-fifths of the Senate votes to limit the debate. In fact, a senator who wants to delay a vote may talk for hours, creating a **filibuster.** The procedure for ending debate in the Senate and taking a vote is called **cloture.**

Is a filibuster beneficial or harmful to the lawmaking process? Why?

Before a bill approved in both houses is sent to the president, it must appear in the same form. If the two houses pass different versions of a bill, a conference committee works to reconcile the two versions. The final version is returned to both houses for a vote.

THE PRESIDENT ACTS ON THE BILL

When a bill reaches the president, he may do one of three things: sign it, **veto** it, or hold it. If he holds it for ten days while Congress is in session, the bill becomes a law. If Congress is not in session, he creates a **pocket veto.** Congress may override a veto with a two-thirds vote in both houses.

Is the process of passing a law simple or complex?

Why do you think lawmakers use this process?

CHALLENGE ACTIVITY

Critical Thinking: Synthesizing Write a bill you would like to introduce to Congress. Then, list arguments for and against your bill for a hearing.

DIRECTIONS Look at each set of terms following each number. On the line provided, write the letter of the term that does not relate to the other terms.

_____ 1. a. money
b. appropriation bill
c. House of Representatives
d. procedure

_____ 2. a. veto
b. committee
c. pocket veto
d. presidential signature

_____ 3. a. House of Representatives
b. filibuster
c. cloture
d. Senate

_____ 4. a. bill
b. act
c. law
d. record

DIRECTIONS Read each sentence and fill in the blank with the term in the word pair that best completes the sentence.

5. After a bill is introduced in the House or the Senate, it is sent to ______________________. (a committee/the president)

6. After a bill is passed in the House, it is sent to the ______________________. (president/Senate)

7. A ______________________ reconciles two versions of the same bill passed by the House and the Senate. (filibuster/conference committee)

8. When a bill reaches the president, he may sign it, ______________________ it, or hold it. (veto/amend)

The Executive Branch

MAIN IDEA

The president and vice president are required to have certain qualifications.

Key Terms

presidential succession the order in which different members of government would replace the president or vice president if he or she could not serve

Academic Vocabulary

role a part or function

Section Summary

THE PRESIDENCY

The United States Constitution states three requirements for a new president. He or she must be born in America. He or she must be at least 35 years old. The president must also have lived in the United States for at least 14 years. The term of office is four years. At first, there was no limit on the number of terms a president could serve. George Washington did not want to serve more than two terms. All presidents who came after him followed his example, until the 1940s. Franklin D. Roosevelt served four terms. In 1951 an amendment changed the Constitution. It limited presidents to only two terms in a row.

How was the Constitution changed to limit the number of terms a president can serve?

____

____

____

The president earns a salary of $400,000, plus extra for expenses and travel costs. Most presidents have been white men who were Christians and had gone to college. Many have been lawyers, and most held some other government office before being elected president. In recent years, more women and members of minority groups have run for president. In 2008 Democratic Senator Barack Obama of Illinois was elected president. He became the first African American to be elected president of the United States.

How was the election of Barack Obama different from other presidential elections?

____

____

THE VICE PRESIDENCY

In the past, the vice president did very little. If the president dies, the vice president takes his place. The president could also leave office or become too sick to serve. In all of these cases, the vice president takes over. He or she does what the president would have done. Eight presidents have died in office. One president left office on his own.

Underline the part of the sentence that tells what happens if the president leaves office.

The Constitution says that vice presidents must be born in the United States. He or she must be at least 35 years old and have lived in this country for 14 years. Vice presidents serve four years. They are paid $230,700 a year. The vice president also has a role in the Senate. He or she votes if there is a tie.

Today, many presidents let their vice presidents help run the country. Vice presidents have gone to other countries to represent the nation. They have worked to get support for the president. Some have even helped with political decisions.

What job does the vice president have in the Senate?

____

____

THE RULES OF SUCCESSION

If the vice president becomes president, a new one is named. The new president appoints the new vice president. The president's choice must be approved by Congress. The Constitution says who replaces the president or vice president if he or she cannot serve. This is called **presidential succession**. The Speaker of the House is third in line for the office. The president pro tempore in the Senate is next. Then members of the president's cabinet follow in the order in which their position was created.

Why is presidential succession important?

____

____

CHALLENGE ACTIVITY

Critical Thinking: Evaluating Consider what the jobs of the president and the vice president are. Write a short paragraph describing which of these jobs you would like to do. Be sure to explain your answer.

role	presidential succession

DIRECTIONS Use the two key terms from the word bank in a summary of what you learned in the section.

____

____

____

____

____

____

____

____

____

DIRECTIONS Read each sentence and fill in the blank with the term in the word pair that best completes the sentence.

1. The ____________________ of the vice president requires that he or she does more than replace the president. (role/ presidential succession)

2. The ____________________ law describes in what order different government officials would replace the president. (role/presidential succession)

MAIN IDEA

The powers and roles of the U.S. president affect not only the citizens of the United States but also people throughout the world.

Key Terms

State of the Union Address a speech that sets forth the programs and policies the president wants Congress to turn into laws

foreign policy the government's plan for interacting with other nations of the world

diplomacy the art of interacting with foreign governments

treaties written agreements with other countries

reprieve an order given by the president to postpone someone's punishment for a crime

pardon an order given by the president that forgives a person for a crime and removes any punishment for it

commutation an order given by the president to reduce a person's punishment

Academic Vocabulary

neutral unbiased, not favoring either side in a conflict

Section Summary

THE PRESIDENT'S ROLES

The Constitution says the president has "executive power." He is head of the Executive Branch of the government. He controls the military forces. He decides how our government deals with other countries. The president also suggest new laws that he wants Congress to pass. Usually in late January, he gives a speech to Congress. This is called the **State of the Union Address**.

This speech tells Congress and the country what the most important issues are. The programs and policies of his term are explained. With this speech, the president also sends a budget. This is a list of how much money the government needs to

Underline the sentences that tell the president's roles.

____

____

function. Congress uses this plan to write laws. The president can veto, or reject, any laws he or she does not agree with. Congress can reject this veto. Two-thirds of both houses of Congress is needed to override the president's veto.

How can the president stop a bill from becoming a law, and how can Congress pass it anyway?

____

____

The commander in chief, or head of the U.S. armed forces, is the president. He or she can order a military leader to do what he says. The president decides how a war will be fought.

The Constitution, however, says only Congress can declare war. The president can send forces anywhere they are needed. But the War Powers Act limits how long the troops can be gone without the approval of Congress.

What role does Congress have in deciding when our military fights a war?

____

____

A nation's **foreign policy** is how its government interacts with other countries. The president sends representatives who use **diplomacy,** or special skills, to have good relations with other countries. The representatives try to remain <u>neutral</u> when their countries fight. They help create **treaties,** or agreements between countries. The Senate advises the president on these treaties. It also gives final approval by a two-thirds vote.

MORE PRESIDENTIAL POWERS

The president names justices to the Supreme Court and other federal courts. A majority of Congress must approve these judges. The president also has the power to change the sentences of people who break federal laws. He or she can grant a reprieve, which postpones punishment. A **commutation** can reduce a person's sentence. A **pardon** forgives someone of a crime and any punishment.

What is the difference between a pardon and a commutation?

____

____

CHALLENGE ACTIVITY

Critical Thinking: Making Judgments Why do you think the president would pardon someone? Write at least two reasons for this kind of forgiveness.

DIRECTIONS Write two adjectives or descriptive phrases that describe the term.

1. treaties ____________________
2. pardons ____________________
3. State of the Union Address ____________________
4. foreign policy ____________________
5. diplomacy ____________________
6. reprieve ____________________

DIRECTIONS Read each sentence and fill in the blank with the term in the word pair that best completes the sentence.

7. Congress wanted to declare war and join one side in the conflict, but the president decided to remain ________________. (neutral/diplomatic)

8. During the ____________________, the president told Congress that he wanted new laws to aid education. (State of the Union Address/diplomacy).

9. The United States signed ________________ with other nations to keep us safe in the world. (pardons/treaties)

10. The president's ________________ allowed a popular politician to leave jail early. (commutation/foreign policy)

DIRECTIONS Look at each set of terms below. On the line provided, write the letter of the term that does not relate to the others.

_____ 1. a. ambassador
b. foreign countries
c. secretary
d. embassy

_____ 2. a. Executive Office of the President
b. Department of Homeland Security
c. Department of State
d. Department of Defense

_____ 3. a. Department of State
b. passports
c. visa
d. military forces

_____ 4. a. Department of Justice
b. foreign business
c. federal laws
d. attorney general

DIRECTIONS Match the terms in the first column with their correct definitions from the second column by placing the letter of the correct definition in the space provided before each term.

_____ 5. Joint Chiefs of Staff

_____ 6. consulate

_____ 7. visas

_____ 8. distinct

_____ 9. consul

_____ 10. Department of Homeland Security

a. separate

b. a place for U.S. business interests in foreign countries

c. the highest-ranking military officers who advise the president

d. its responsibility is to protect the nation against terrorists attacks

e. a representative of U.S. business in other countries

f. a legal document given to foreigners who come to America

Name ______________________ Class ______________ Date ______________

The Executive Branch

Section 4

MAIN IDEA

The independent agencies and regulatory commissions of the U.S. government perform specialized duties.

Key Terms

independent agencies government bodies created by Congress to do a special job

regulatory commission an independent agency that has the power to make rules

bureaucracy the employees of commissions, agencies, and other departments

Academic Vocabulary

established set up or created

Section Summary

INDEPENDENT AGENCIES

Congress created 65 **independent agencies** in the government to do special jobs. For example, the U.S. Commission on Civil Rights gathers data about discrimination aimed at minorities. The National Aeronautics and Space Administration (NASA) runs the U.S. space program.

Some agencies help to run the federal government. The Office of Personnel Management tests people who want to work for the government. The General Services Administration buys what the government needs.

Underline what the Office of Personnel Management does.

REGULATORY COMMISSIONS

A **regulatory commission** is a type of government agency. It creates rules. It also brings those who break the rules to court. The decisions these bodies make act like laws.

Congress established a regulatory commission to determine if federal elections were fair. It passed a law to create the Federal Election Commission. This group makes sure the law is obeyed. It controls how money is spent on elections.

How could a commission's decision act like a law?

____

____

Another example is the Consumer Product Safety Commission. It makes sure products sold in stores and online are safe. The Securities and Exchange Commission makes sure the laws controlling stocks and bonds are followed. Federal labor laws are the concern of the National Labor Relations Board. The board also makes sure that businesses deal with each other fairly.

The president names the heads of these regulatory commissions. The heads have a lot of freedom because they do not have to take orders from different parts of the government. This gives the commissions more power. Also, the heads do not just leave office after a new president is elected. They often serve under many presidents. Each president can appoint a few heads, and then the Senate must approve them.

How does having freedom affect the work of regulatory commissions?

____

____

Critics of these commissions say they have too much power. Others believe they protect the public.

THE FEDERAL BUREAUCRACY

The federal **bureaucracy** describes all the employees of the executive departments and these agencies. It numbers more than 3 million people. Some citizens complain that the bureaucracy makes and enforces too many rules. Often two departments have control over the same area, and this causes confusion. Some people complain about too many forms to fill out and long lines. Others say that the government is run very well, and that without this bureaucracy, life would be unfair. The departments and agencies protect ordinary citizens from those who would misuse the government.

Which argument about the federal bureaucracy do you support? Why?

____

____

CHALLENGE ACTIVITY

Critical Thinking: Comparing and Contrasting

Write a short essay comparing and contrasting the independent agencies and the regulatory commissions.

independent agencies	regulatory commission	bureaucracy
established		

DIRECTIONS Answer each question by writing a sentence that contains at least one term from the word bank.

1. What argument do some people make about all of the agencies and executive departments of the federal government?

____

____

____

2. What type of government agency has the power to make rules that are almost laws?

____

____

____

3. What did Congress create to do special jobs in our government?

____

____

____

4. Explain who created the regulatory agencies and why.

____

____

____

Name ______________________ Class ______________ Date ______________

MAIN IDEA

The rights of all U.S. citizens are protected by laws and the courts.

Key Terms

crime any behavior that is illegal because society, through its government, considers the behavior harmful to society

criminal law refers to the group of laws that define what acts are crimes

civil law is the group of laws that refer to disputes between people

common law is a type of law that comes from judges' decisions that rely on common sense and previous cases

precedent an earlier court decision that a judge follows

constitutional law is based on the constitution and Supreme Court decisions interpreting the constitution

appeal the process by which the person asks a higher court to review the result of the trial

Academic Vocabulary

affect to change or influence

Section Summary

A NATION OF LAWS

Every society or nation needs rules. Laws are the rules of a nation. Laws set limits or boundaries on behavior. When those limits are broken, a **crime** has been committed. There are two basic types of law—criminal law and civil law.

What are the two basic types of law?

____

____

____

Criminal law refers to laws that state which acts are crimes. These laws also describe how a person accused of a crime is to be tried in court and what punishment they should receive.

Civil law is a group of laws that refers to disputes between people. Civil laws settle personal issues

Why are criminal laws established?

____

____

like divorce and contract and property disputes. People can go to court and get their disputes settled.

SOURCES OF LAW

There are several sources of law in the United States. One source is statutory law. These are laws passed by Congress or state and local governments. Most criminal laws are statutory laws. Many civil laws are statutory laws.

Common law is law that comes from a judge's decision. To make the decision, the judge considers customs and traditions. A judge also considers similar legal cases that have been decided before. This is called the **precedent** or earlier decision.

Laws that influence or affect our daily lives are created by government agencies. They are called administrative laws. These laws cover, for example, health and safety issues and education and banking.

The group of laws that determine how men and women in the military behave is called the *Uniform Code of Military Justice*. This code includes laws for specific military issues like desertion.

The Constitution is the law with the greatest authority in the U.S. The Supreme Court interprets the Constitution and creates c**onstitutional law.**

What are three things a judge considers in making a decision involving common law?

____

____

____

What law does the Supreme Court interpret?

____

____

____

THE ROLE OF THE COURTS

All courts use the law to settle disputes. Everyone has a right to an attorney and the right to **appeal** a court decision. In criminal cases, the accused is innocent until proven guilty, has a right to trial by jury, and the right to confront the accuser.

CHALLENGE ACTIVITY

Critical Thinking: Elaborating Imagine you are a lawyer. Write four paragraphs about the kind of cases you work on. Explain whether they are criminal or civil law cases.

common law	crime	constitutional law	precedent
appeal	affect	civil law	criminal law

DIRECTIONS On the line provided before each statement, write **T** if a statement is true or **F** if a statement is false. If the statement is false, find a word or phrase in the word bank that makes the statement true. Write a new sentence on the line provided.

_____ 1. Criminal law deals with disputes between people, like divorce.

____

_____ 2. Constitutional law is created by the Supreme Court interpreting the Constitution.

____

_____ 3. Everyone has the right to appeal the verdict of their case.

____

_____ 4. A court decision that takes into consideration earlier decisions made about crimes is called common law.

____

_____ 5. Laws that affect our daily lives are administrative laws.

____

_____ 6. Civil law deals with crimes.

____

Name ______________________ Class ______________ Date ______________

MAIN IDEA

The federal court system consists of three levels of courts, each of which has specific duties.

Key Terms

jurisdiction the range of authority the court has to hear and decide a case that has been properly brought before it.

district courts trial courts that make up the lowest level of federal courts

original jurisdiction the power of a court to hear and decide a case for the first time

courts of appeals the second level of federal courts; handles appeals

appellate jurisdiction a court that has the power to review decisions made by a lower court

justices the nine judges of the Supreme Court

Academic Vocabulary

authority the power or right to rule

Section Summary

U.S. DISTRICT COURTS

The three levels of the federal court system that have **jurisdiction** over the United States are the district courts, the appeals courts, and the Supreme Court.

The **district courts** are the courts of **original jurisdiction**. They hear and decide a case for the first time. District courts are the only federal courts in which jury trials are held.

Which federal court hears and decides a case for the first time?

____

____

Every state, including the District of Columbia, has at least one district court. Some states have more than one. There are 94 federal district courts in the United States.

Federal district judges apply laws to the facts of the cases before them. They hear cases that involve civil and criminal cases with or without juries.

If there is no jury, the judge decides who wins and the remedy for the winner. The judge decides the punishment in a criminal case.

Federal judges are appointed by the president and approved by the Senate. Only impeachment by Congress can remove a federal judge. The salary of a judge cannot be changed while in office. This is included in the U.S. Constitution to guarantee that judges are not punished for their decisions.

What law protects U.S. federal judges from being punished for their decisions?

____

____

U.S. COURTS OF APPEALS

If the person who lost in the district court wants to appeal their case, they can go to the **courts of appeals**. This court has **appellate jurisdiction.** This means it can review decisions made by the district courts.

Trials are not held in the courts of appeals. A panel of at least three judges reviews the records of the earlier trial. They hear arguments from lawyers representing both sides. The judges decide whether the original trial was fair. They decide if the law was interpreted correctly. They reach their decision by a majority vote. Usually the appeals court decision is final.

How are decisions reached in the courts of appeals?

____

____

____

THE U.S. SUPREME COURT

The U.S. Supreme Court is the final authority. It meets in Washington, D.C. It is the last court for appeal. It reviews cases tried in the district courts and reviewed by the appellate courts. The decisions by the nine **justices** cannot be appealed.

The Supreme Court has original jurisdiction for three types of cases. It hears cases involving foreign diplomats, cases between states, and cases between a state and the federal government.

What court hears cases between states?

____

____

CHALLENGE ACTIVITY

Critical Thinking: Developing Questions

Develop three questions about the U.S. district courts. Write the answers to your questions.

jurisdiction	authority	district courts
original jurisdiction	courts of appeals	appellate jurisdiction
justices		

DIRECTIONS Answer each question by writing a sentence that contains at least one term from the word bank.

1. What court does a person accused of a criminal act first appear in?

____

____

2. What authority do the district courts have that the courts of appeals do not have?

____

____

3. Who decides cases in the Supreme Court?

____

____

4. What is another name for the appellate courts?

____

____

5. What does the Supreme Court have that is final?

____

____

DIRECTIONS Choose at least five of the key terms from the word bank. On a separate sheet of paper, use these words to write three paragraphs that explain the three levels of U.S. courts.

MAIN IDEA

The Supreme Court hears appeals, reviews laws, and strongly influences American society.

Key Terms

judicial review a court's authority to decide whether a law or presidential action is in agreement with the U.S. Constitution

remand the return by the Supreme Court of a case to a lower court for retrial

opinion an explanation of the reasoning behind a decision by the Supreme Court

concurring opinion when a justice agrees with the majority opinion but for different reasons

dissenting opinion when a justice believes the majority opinion is wrong

Academic Vocabulary

explicitly states in detail

Section Summary

THE POWER OF JUDICIAL REVIEW

The Supreme Court holds the authority **of judicial review**, deciding whether a law is constitutional. The right of judicial review is not explicitly stated in the U.S. Constitution. It evolved from the 1803 court case, *Marbury* v. *Madison*. The Court established judicial review by declaring the law in question, the Judiciary Act of 1789, unconstitutional.

What power does the Supreme Court have that is not explicitly stated in the U.S. Constitution?

____

____

____

The Supreme Court reviews only cases that deal with constitutional and national questions. The Court accepts only about 100 cases per year. Four justices must vote to hear a case. If the Court refuses to consider a case, the lower court decision stands. The Court can **remand** a case to a lower court for retrial.

Justices hear oral and written arguments. After considering the arguments, they meet in private to vote. Decisions are reached by a majority vote. The Court delivers its **opinion** to explain its decision publicly. The Court's opinion is binding on all lower courts. Justices can write a **concurring opinion** if they agree with the decision but have different reasons for doing so. Justices who disagree with the majority write a **dissenting opinion**.

Congress decides the number of justices, but since 1869 there have been nine. There is a chief justice and eight associates. They are appointed for life by the president and approved by the Senate. Justices can be removed only by impeachment.

What is the difference between a concurring opinion and a dissenting opinion?

____

____

____

CHECKING THE COURT'S POWER

The executive branch and legislative branch can check the power of the Supreme Court. The president nominates a justice and the Senate must confirm the appointment. If the Court declares a law unconstitutional, Congress can re-write the law. Or the Constitution can be amended.

What elected body must confirm the presidential nomination of a justice?

____

____

____

STRENGTHENING RIGHTS

Supreme Court decisions have enabled the Constitution to meet the needs of changing times. In *Brown* v. *Board of Education* (1954), the Court said that segregated schools were unequal and violated the Fourteenth Amendment. This reversed *Plessy* v. *Ferguson* (1896) which had legalized segregation.

Supreme Court decisions involving voting rights and the rights of the accused have also made significant changes in American life.

What Court decision in the twentieth century reversed a 1896 court decision?

____

____

CHALLENGE ACTIVITY

Critical Thinking: Sequencing Create a time line of events regarding the Supreme Court. Describe each of the events and explain how one event caused or resulted from another event.

DIRECTIONS Match the terms in the first column with their correct definitions from the second column by placing the letter of the correct definition in the space provided before each term.

_____ 1. dissenting opinion

_____ 2. remand

_____ 3. judicial review

_____ 4. opinion

_____ 5. explicitly

_____ 6. concurring opinion

a. an explanation of the reasoning behind a decision by the Supreme Court

b. the power the Court has to decide whether a presidential action or a law is in agreement with the U.S. Constitution

c. when a justice disagrees with the majority opinion

d. the return by the Supreme Court of a case to a lower court for retrial

e. states in detail

f. when a justice agrees with the majority opinion but has different reasons than expressed in the Court opinion

Name ______________________ Class ______________ Date ____________

State Government

Section 1

MAIN IDEA

In the United States, all 50 independent states fit together to form one country. The federal system allows state governments to serve the needs of their citizens while cooperating as a united country.

Key Terms

delegated powers powers given to the federal government

reserved powers any power not delegated to the federal government; belong to the people and the states

concurrent powers powers shared by both state and federal governments

full faith and credit clause part of the Constitution that ensures that each state will accept the decisions of civil courts in other states

extradition the process of returning fugitives

Section Summary

STATE GOVERNMENT POWERS

The 13 states agreed to join together as one nation when they ratified the Constitution. However, they did not want the new federal government to become too powerful. To prevent this, they set up a federal system of government. This system divides powers between the federal and state governments.

Why did the states set up a federal system of government?

____

____

The powers given to the federal government are called **delegated powers.** These powers include printing money and carrying out foreign policy. Other powers are granted to the state governments only. The Constitution states that any power not delegated to the federal government belongs to the people and the states. These powers are called **reserved powers.**

How do delegated powers differ from reserved powers?

____

____

Reserved powers let state governments pass laws that protect the health, safety, and welfare of the people. States also run education systems and carry out elections. In addition, states have authority over local governments found within their boundaries. These local governments include cities, counties, and districts.

State and federal governments also share some powers. These are known as **concurrent powers.** The power to tax citizens is an example of a concurrent power. State and national governments also share the authority to make and enforce laws. Like the national government, states have legislatures that create and pass new laws. Most states also have a state police force to help enforce these laws.

Name two concurrent powers in the U.S. federal system.

____

____

Each state government has its own constitution. These documents list the rules to create each state's government. These documents usually explain how a state government is organized. They also tell how to run elections, how to manage state affairs, and how to amend the state constitution.

OUR FEDERAL SYSTEM

Our federal system requires states to work together with each other and the federal government. Article IV, Section 1 of the U.S. Constitution includes the **full faith and credit clause.** This requires states to accept the decisions of civil courts in other states. For example, official records from one state must be accepted in all other states. States also work together through **extradition.** This is the process of returning fugitives. It means, for example, that a person who steals a car in Utah and flees to Arizona can be returned to Utah for trial.

Underline the statement that explains the full faith and credit clause.

States work with the federal government to share the costs of important social services, such as building roads or helping the unemployed. These governments also cooperate to help people in times of crisis.

CHALLENGE ACTIVITY

Critical Thinking: Evaluating Think about a project or problem in your community on which the state and federal government might work together. Write a letter to the editor in which you describe this issue and explain how the governments might work together successfully on it.

delegated powers	concurrent powers	extradition
reserved powers	full faith and credit clause	

DIRECTIONS Write an adjective or descriptive phrase that describes the term given.

1. delegated powers ______________________
2. reserved powers ______________________
3. concurrent powers ______________________
4. full faith and credit clause ______________________
5. extradition ______________________

DIRECTIONS Read each sentence and fill in the blank with the term from the word bank that best completes the sentence.

6. Printing money and carrying out foreign policy are two examples of ______________________.
7. The ______________________ requires that official records from one state must be accepted in all other states.
8. ______________________ require the federal and state governments to work together.
9. Through ______________________, a fugitive that flees to another state can be returned to the state where his crime occurred to stand trial.
10. Any power not directly granted to the federal government is considered one of the ______________________, and belongs to the states and the people.

MAIN IDEA

The process of passing state laws is similar to the process used in the U.S. Congress. In some states, citizens can take a direct role in making the state's laws.

Key Terms

bicameral divided into two houses

unicameral made up of a single house

constituents the citizens represented by lawmakers

initiative a process through which citizens can initiate legislation

referendum a method of referring potential laws directly to the people for approval

recall a process by which voters can remove elected officials from office

Academic Vocabulary

develop create

Section Summary

STATE LEGISLATURES

Every state has a lawmaking body, or legislature. People elect lawmakers, or legislators, to make laws on their behalf. Most state legislatures are made up of two houses. These are called **bicameral** legislatures. Nebraska is the only state to have a **unicameral** legislature. This means it has only a single house.

How many houses does a bicameral legislature have?

____

____

The size of state legislatures varies greatly. However, they are all organized to give citizens equal representation. This is done by dividing states into areas called legislative districts. Each legislator represents the people who live in one district. These districts must be nearly equal in population to guarantee the principle of "one person, one vote."

People must meet certain qualifications to become state legislators. Most states require legislators to be U.S. citizens, live in the district they represent, and be at least a certain age.

Underline the qualifications that most states require state legislators to meet.

Legislators all serve for a specific term, or period of time. Fewer than a third of states place limits on the number of terms legislators can serve.

Legislators also receive payment and benefits for their work. These vary greatly across states. Each state has a schedule for when its legislature meets. Legislators choose leaders for each new session.

PASSING STATE LAWS

States pass laws that govern all areas within their responsibility. The lawmaking process of states is similar to that of Congress. A bill is introduced by a legislator, then sent to committee. If the committee approves it, the bill reaches the floor. If the first house passes the bill, it is sent to the second house. There, it follows the same steps as in the first house. Bills must pass both houses to become law. The bill finally becomes a law when the governor signs it.

What is the final step for a bill to become a state law?

____

____

HOW CITIZENS PARTICIPATE IN LAWMAKING

Citizens can participate in state lawmaking in a number of ways. Many legislators appreciate input from their **constituents,** or citizens they represent. Citizens can help develop state laws. They can speak at committee meetings, send letters and make phone calls, or attend meetings of the legislature.

In some states, people can make laws themselves through a process called the **initiative.** Citizens must propose a law and collect enough voter signatures for their proposed law to appear on the ballot. A **referendum** allows voters to approve bills passed by the legislature. A process known as **recall** allows voters to use a petition to remove elected officials from office.

Circle the term that that allows voters to remove elected officials from office.

CHALLENGE ACTIVITY

Critical Thinking: Making Judgments Do citizens in your state effectively participate in lawmaking? Write a paragraph in which you state and explain your position.

bicameral	initiative	develop
unicameral	referendum	constituents
recall		

DIRECTIONS On the line provided before each statement, write **T** if a statement is true and **F** if a statement is false. If the statement is false, rewrite it as a true statement on the line.

_____ 1. Nebraska is one of many states that has a unicameral legislature.

____

_____ 2. Constituents are the people who make up state legislative bodies.

____

_____ 3. Citizens can make laws themselves through the initiative.

____

_____ 4. A bicameral legislature is made up of only a single house.

____

_____ 5. Citizens can remove elected officials from office using a process known as recall.

____

_____ 6. A referendum allows voters to add new members to the state legislature.

____

_____ 7. Citizens often help to develop laws.

____

Name ______________ Class ______________ Date ______________

MAIN IDEA

A state's executive branch carries out laws made by the state's legislative branch. Governors are the chief executives of state government.

Key Terms

governor the chief executive in each state

patronage giving state jobs to people recommended by political party leaders

lieutenant governor state executive official that becomes head of the executive branch if the governor dies, resigns, or is removed from office

Section Summary

THE STATE'S CHIEF EXECUTIVE

The **governor** is the chief executive in each state. The citizens of each state elect a governor to lead the state government. Governors handle the day-to-day business of the states.

> **How do states choose their governors?**
>
> ______________
>
> ______________

States' constitutions list the qualifications for governors. Most governors must be U.S. citizens and have lived in their states for a certain period of time. Most governors must also be at least 30 years old. Governors usually serve four-year terms. About half of the states limit them to one or two terms.

Governors receive a wide range of salaries. States also usually pay for governors' expenses. Most governors and their families live in an official home in the state capital.

The governor leads a state's executive branch. He or she carries out the state's laws. To do this, a governor has three main roles: chief executive, chief legislator, and political party leader.

> **Circle the three main roles that each governor has as the leader of a state's executive branch.**

As chief executive, the governor has several important powers. He or she makes the state's budget. This budget determines what is important to the state. The governor also appoints citizens to work for state agencies. These agencies help the governor carry out laws and serve the state. State agencies handle things like agriculture, transportation, and public safety. The governor also supervises the work of these agencies. Most state government jobs are open to all citizens. However, some jobs are filled through **patronage.** This means that jobs are given to people recommended by political party leaders. These are often people who have helped with an election campaign.

As chief legislator, the governor proposes new laws to the legislature. Only the legislature can make laws, but the governor can suggest laws that he or she thinks should be passed. The governor can also veto a bill that he or she opposes.

Underline the sentence that summarizes how governors work as chief legislators.

The governor also serves as the leader of his or her political party in the state. State legislators often model their ideas after the governor's. The governor can also help campaign during state elections.

OTHER STATE EXECUTIVE OFFICIALS

Each state has other officials that help the governor run the state government. In most states, voters elect these officials. In others, the governor appoints them. For instance, a **lieutenant governor** becomes head of the state executive branch if the governor dies, resigns, or is removed from office.

Other officials include the secretary of state. This person keeps records and carries out elections. The attorney general handles the legal business of the state. A state treasurer manages a state's money. He or she might supervise taxes and paying the state's bills. State auditors study states' financial records to make sure they are correct. Another term for auditor is *comptroller*. Finally, the superintendent of public instruction is in charge of education in the state.

Which state executive official is responsible for handling a state's legal business?

____

____

CHALLENGE ACTIVITY

Critical Thinking: Analyzing Suppose you could work as any of the executive officials described in this lesson. Write a brief paragraph explaining which role you would choose and why.

governor	patronage	lieutenant governor

DIRECTIONS Answer each question by writing a sentence that contains at least one term from the word bank.

1. Who is the leader of the state's executive branch? What three roles does this official have?

____

____

2. What is one way that citizens can gain jobs in the state government?

____

____

3. What is another example of a state executive official? What is the role of this official?

____

____

MAIN IDEA

State court systems include lower courts, general trial courts, appeals courts, and state supreme courts.

Key Terms

penal code a set of criminal laws

Missouri Plan a method of selecting judges in which the governor appoints a judge from a list of qualified judges prepared by a committee of judges, lawyers, and ordinary citizens

Section Summary

STATE COURT CASES

Citizens are subject to two levels of law and two judicial systems. Federal courts deal with violations of the United States Constitution and federal laws. State courts handle violations of state constitutions and state laws. Each state can set up its own court system. It can also decide how judges are chosen. However, all state court systems must apply and enforce the laws of the state.

Each state has a **penal code.** This is a set of criminal laws. State lawyers prosecute people accused of committing crimes. State judges hear these cases. If a person is guilty, the state court can punish that person. State courts also hear civil law cases, or disagreements over money or property.

What is a penal code?

____

____

STATE COURT SYSTEM

State court systems have different levels. Most states have three types of courts: general trial courts, appeals courts, and a state supreme court.

Lower trial courts usually hear minor cases. These could include small criminal offenses and civil cases involving small amounts of money. Major criminal and civil cases are heard in general trial courts. A jury decides most of these cases, while a judge presides over the trials.

Underline the three different levels of state courts.

If a person believes his or her case was handled unfairly, he or she may appeal the decision to an appeals court. This court may reconsider the case. This usually happens if a person's right to a fair trial was violated. Appeals court judges study what happened in the lower court. They hear arguments from both sides' lawyers and make a decision. If a person disagrees with appeals court's decision, he or she can then appeal to the state supreme court.

Who decides a case in a state appeals court?

____

____

The state supreme court is most states' highest court. Like the U.S. Supreme Court, these judges hear cases on appeal. A state supreme court's decision on state law is final.

SELECTION OF STATE JUDGES

Citizens elect state supreme court judges in most states. In others, the governor appoints these judges. Each state decides how its judges are selected and how long they can serve.

Some people believe that electing judges makes the judges responsible to the people of the state. People who favor electing judges also fear that governors might appoint their friends and supporters as judges.

Opponents of elections believe that judges should decide cases based on the law, and not on what might win voters. These people believe that judges should be appointed based on their skills. Some states pick judges using the **Missouri Plan.** Under this plan, a committee of judges, lawyers, and ordinary citizens make a list of qualified judges. The governor then appoints a judge from the list. People can vote on these judges in the next election.

Who shares the responsibility for choosing judges under the Missouri Plan?

____

____

CHALLENGE ACTIVITY

Critical Thinking: Elaborating Prepare a short oral presentation in which you elaborate on the steps that a case could follow in the state court system, from trial courts to the state supreme court.

DIRECTIONS Write two adjectives or descriptive phrases that describe the term.

1. penal code ____

2. Missouri Plan ____

DIRECTIONS Read each sentence and fill in the blank with the key term in the word pair that best completes the sentence.

3. Each state is responsible for creating its own ________________________ for prosecuting criminals. (penal code/Missouri Plan)

4. Some states have adopted the ______________________ as a method of selecting judges for the state court system. (penal code/Missouri Plan)

Section 1

MAIN IDEA

Local governments have grown as the country has grown. As Americans settled in rural communities, towns, cities, and suburbs, they set up local governments.

Key Terms and People

municipality a unit of local government that is incorporated by the state and that has a large degree of self-government.

city the largest type of municipality

county a division of state government formed to carry out specific state laws

sheriff an elected county official in charge of law enforcement

charter a basic plan that defines the powers and responsibilities of a local government

ordinances regulations that govern a local community

Section Summary

ESTABLISHING LOCAL GOVERNMENTS

States use their power to incorporate, or officially establish, various types of local governments. Any unit of local government is called a **municipality**. A **city** is the largest type of municipality.

Local governments provide the services that residents expect in their everyday life, such as maintaining roads, water systems, and school safety. Police and firefighters may also be part of local government. Local governments are often responsible for running local schools.

What is the relationship between a municipality and a city?

____

____

COUNTY GOVERNMENTS

A **county** is the highest level of local government within a state. County government carries out state laws, collects certain taxes, runs elections, and so on. County employees provide health care, welfare, corrections, and other services.

Voters elect the members of county government, called county commissioners or the county board.

County officials have the power to pass certain laws that pertain to the county. They also set and collect real estate and school taxes. Members of county government work together to help the county run well. There is usually no one person at the head of county government.

The **sheriff** runs the county's law enforcement operations. The sheriff and his or her employees make arrests and carry out orders from the county courts. Other county officials include the county clerk, who keeps a record of county meetings, and the county treasurer, who keeps track of the county's money.

Underline the words that tell what the sheriff is in charge of.

GOVERNMENTS WORK TOGETHER

A **charter** is a state-approved plan that outlines the powers and responsibilities of a local government. The local government is responsible for making its community a better place to live. Local governments pass **ordinances**, or regulations, that help to improve life in the community. Ordinances cannot conflict with state law or federal law. Ordinances are enforced by local law enforcement.

What are local regulations called?

____

____

Local governments help the state by organizing and running elections according to state law. They also set up polling places where people vote. Without this local organization, elections could not take place.

CHALLENGE ACTIVITY

Critical Thinking: Evaluating Think about one local law in your town or city that you would like to change. Why do you want to change it? How would you go about trying to get it changed?

DIRECTIONS Read each sentence and fill in the blank with the word in the word pair that best completes the sentence.

1. A ____________ is a place in a state that has a relatively large urban population. (county/city)

2. A ____________ government is run by a board or commission, not by a single head of government. (county/city)

3. An incorporated local government, called a ______________, has a large degree of self-government. (charter/municipality)

4. Its ____________ outlines the basic powers and responsibilities of a local government. (charter/ordinance)

5. The county ________________ is in charge of enforcing laws and court orders. (charter/sheriff)

6. Local government has the power to pass __________________ to improve the lives of local citizens. (ordinances/charters)

Name ______________________ Class ______________ Date ______________

Local Government

Section 2

MAIN IDEA

Although counties are the largest unit of local government, they share the job of governing with other units of local government.

Key Terms

town a unit of local government that is usually larger than a village but smaller than a city

town meeting a regularly held meeting where all town citizens discuss town issues

township an often smaller type of town

special district a unit of government formed to meet many different needs, such as fire protection, public transportation, libraries, etc.

Section Summary

TOWN GOVERNMENT

Towns date from colonial times in New England. A **town** is a unit of local government generally larger than a village and smaller than a city. In colonial New England, towns began to use town meetings to govern the towns. A **town meeting** is a regularly scheduled meeting of all town citizens to discuss town issues. Decisions are made by a vote of all the citizens at the meeting.

Circle the sentence that tells you how decisions are made at town meetings.

Town meetings are often the site of town elections. At an election meeting, townspeople usually elect three to five officials to manage the town between meetings. Town meetings are one of the best examples of direct democracy because everyone takes a direct part in solving problems and electing officials.

TOWNSHIPS AND SPECIAL DISTRICTS

Townships are another unit of local government that date back to colonial times. A **township** is similar to a town. New England townships were usually smaller than towns. In the Midwest, townships may have been larger than some other towns. Townships perform many of the same functions as towns, such as building schools and roads. Most townships have a commissioner or board of trustees to run the local government. A justice of the peace often tries minor cases.

A special district may be created to provide citizens with a variety of services, such as fire fighting, libraries, parks, and sewage treatment. A **special district** is a unit of local government that is established by the state legislature through a charter. The legislature often sets up a commission to run the special district and make sure it is providing needed services. In some areas, school districts are considered special districts. These districts provide education to a wide area, which may include several towns.

What are two services a special district may provide?

____

____

VILLAGE AND BOROUGH GOVERNMENTS

A rural community that grows to 200 to 300 households may find it necessary to work together to establish a village or borough. In this way, they can create their own local government. Residents must get the approval of the state legislature before they can establish a village or borough. Once the local government is established, it can collect taxes, have its own police and firefighters, and provide other services to residents. Most villages or boroughs are governed by elected councils or boards.

Who must approve the formation of a village or borough?

____

____

CHALLENGE ACTIVITY

Critical Thinking: Analyzing The town meeting is an example of direct democracy, involving all citizens in government. Do you think town meetings should be expanded to cities, where "neighborhood meetings" would involve citizens directly in government? Explain whether or not you think neighborhood meetings are a good idea for city government.

township	town	town meeting
special district		

DIRECTIONS Read each sentence and fill in the blank with the word or phrase from the word bank that best completes the sentence.

1. A school district is a form of ________________ whose function is to provide education to the citizens in an area.
2. As the United States was being settled, a ________________ in the Midwest was often larger than the same form of local government in New England.
3. The earliest form of local government in America was the ________________, which was established by citizens living in New England.
4. A ________________ is a place where every citizen can speak his or her mind about how local problems should be solved.

DIRECTIONS How are towns, townships, special districts, villages, and boroughs alike? How are they different? Write a brief paragraph comparing these forms of local government.

____

____

____

____

____

____

____

____

____

Name ______________________ Class ______________ Date ______________

Local Government

Section 3

MAIN IDEA

A city is usually larger than a town or village. In many cities, a large population is crowded into a relatively small area, which creates many challenges for city government.

Key Terms

home rule a state regulation that allows city government to write and change its own charter

city council the legislative body in city government

mayor the chief executive of a city

commission three to nine elected officials who act as a city's legislature and executive

Academic Vocabulary

primary main, most important

Section Summary

HOME RULE ORGANIZATION

Cities are the largest municipalities, but cities vary in size. Traditionally, a city received a charter from the state legislature that gave the city the right to self-government. Today, however, many cities have been given home rule by their state government. **Home rule** allows the city to write and change its own charter, with the approval of the voters.

Circle the sentence that explains what home rule allows a city to do.

FORMS OF CITY GOVERNMENT

A city's charter describes the type of government the city has. The oldest and most common form of city government is the mayor-council system. The **city council** is the legislative body in city government. The **mayor** is the chief executive. Together they govern the city.

A city may be divided into wards, or districts, with each ward electing a representative to the city council. Everyone in the city elects the mayor.

A city with a weak-mayor government gives most governing power to the city council. A city that has a strong-mayor government gives more power to the mayor. The mayor has the primary responsibility for running the city.

Around 1900, the city of Galveston, Texas, created a new form of city government called the commission. In the **commission** form of government, the city is governed by three to nine elected officials, or commissioners. The commission acts like a legislature, passing laws. The commission also acts as the city's executive body. Each commissioner is head of one city department, such as police, fire, education, or transportation. Each commission head is responsible for the efficient running of the department.

How are a city council and a commission the same in terms of their function?

____

____

The council-manager form of city government is a commission form of government with a city manager added. The voters elect the city council. Then the council members choose the manager. The city manager is like a mayor, appointing department heads and overseeing the running of city government.

Some people think this form of city government works well because the city manager must do a good job or the council can fire her or him. Other people think this is not a good form of government because the people do not elect the manager directly.

CHALLENGE ACTIVITY

Critical Thinking: Summarizing Most city governments have a legislative body. Many have an executive. Create a chart that summarizes the main characteristics of each form of city government.

DIRECTIONS Match the definition with the correct term from the right column.

_____	1. This is the legislative body in a city government whose members are elected by residents in different wards or districts of the city.	a. commission
_____	2. This is the right given by the state that allows a city to change its municipal charter.	b. home rule
_____	3. In this form of city government, three to nine elected officials act as both legislature and executive.	c. mayor
_____	4. This person is the chief executive in city government.	d. city council

DIRECTIONS Write two adjectives or descriptive phrases that describe each term below.

5. mayor ____

6. commission ____

7. city council ____

8. home rule ____

9. primary ____

Name ______________________ Class ____________ Date ____________

Local Government

Section 4

MAIN IDEA

You live under three levels of government—local, state, and federal. Without cooperation among these levels, everyday life would not run smoothly.

Key Terms

grants-in-aid federal funds given to state and local governments to be spent for a specific purpose

block grants federal funds given to state and local governments for more broadly defined, less specific purposes

Academic Vocabulary

implement to put in place; to enact or carry out

Section Summary

GOVERNMENTS WORK TOGETHER

States grant cities and smaller municipalities the right to govern themselves. Under our federal system of government, the power of each level of government is clearly defined. All levels of government must follow the U.S. Constitution. State constitutions set out the powers of the state and of the cities, towns, and villages within the state.

Circle the name of the document that all governments must follow.

Each level of government has its own power, yet every level of government must cooperate for life to run smoothly. For example, all three levels of government—federal, state, and local—have the responsibility to maintain roads. As all roads eventually connect with other roads, every level of government must uphold its responsibility. If one level of government neglects its responsibility, the roads will suffer and citizens will have difficulty using the roads. Today every state has a network of roads built with local, state, and federal money.

GOVERNMENTS COOPERATE TO SERVE THE PUBLIC

All levels of government must cooperate to provide the services citizens need. For example, state governments help counties and cities pay for schools and education costs, while state education boards set educational standards that schools must follow. The federal government provides funds to states, and sometimes to cities, to help pay for education.

The federal government helps state and local governments implement, or carry out, laws and programs by providing them with money. **Grants-in-aid** are federal funds given to a state or local government to carry out a specific project. The state or local government must meet certain conditions before the money is given out. Sometimes, the state must provide some of its own fund for the project.

Circle the sentence that describes what a grant-in-aid is for.

Block grants are federal funds given to state and local governments for more broadly defined purposes. Block grants may be used to pay for whatever the state or locality thinks is important.

States also work with local governments to improve the quality of life. States license businesses and professionals, regulate health care, set education standards, etc.

GOVERNMENTS IN COMPETITION

Governments at every level also compete, particularly for tax dollars. States compete with each other to attract businesses and jobs. Cities also compete for businesses. Both cooperation and competition keep all levels of government efficient and responsive to citizens' needs.

What is one thing states compete for?

____

____

CHALLENGE ACTIVITY

Critical Thinking: Making Inferences Why might it benefit states and cities to compete for businesses that will bring jobs? In what ways might this form of competition be harmful to states and cities?

DIRECTIONS Read each sentence and fill in the blank with the term in the word pair that best completes the sentence.

1. The federal government helps state governments ______________________ programs by giving them money. (grant-in-aid/implement)

2. A locality may use a ____________________ to pay for any project that the locality finds important. (block grant/grant-in-aid)

DIRECTIONS Under what conditions would the federal government prefer to give states or localities a grant-in-aid rather than a block grant? Write a paragraph explaining your answer.

____

____

____

____

____

____

____

____

____

____

Name ______________________ Class ______________ Date ______________

Electing Leaders

Section 1

MAIN IDEA

Political parties play an important role in the American democratic process. Party supporters put their political ideas to work at all levels of government.

Key Terms

political party a group of people with similar views on public matters

nominate to select a candidate to run for a political office

candidate person who runs for a government office

political spectrum the range of differences in views between political parties

two-party system government dominated by two main political parties

multiparty system government run by more than two strong political parties

coalition parties in a multiparty system working together to run the government

one-party system government controlled by a single strong political party

third parties additional parties in what is normally a two-party system

Academic Vocabulary

impact an effect or result

Section Summary

POLITICAL PARTIES

A group of citizens with shared views on public matters and which works together to turn their views into government action is a **political party**. An important way of achieving government action is to **nominate** a **candidate** from their party to run for office. This person represents the views held by most members of the political party. In the United States, ideas shared by members of the two main political parties represent a range of political views. These views can be said to spread across the **political spectrum**. The two parties share some views, but vary on many important matters.

What does a candidate do?

____

____

THE TWO-PARTY SYSTEM

Although there are many political parties in the United States, this country is said to have a **two-party system**. This is because two main parties—the Democrats and the Republicans—dominate our government. Governments in countries that use a **multiparty system** sometimes have difficulty when members of the many parties cannot agree. When they do compromise and agree to cooperate, the different parties have formed a **coalition**. In some countries no opportunity for such cooperation exists. Countries with a **one-party system** have a single political party that dominates the government. Often the government outlaws competing political parties.

THIRD PARTIES

In modern times, two political parties have dominated the U.S. government. This does not mean that the other political parties have been without impact. Sometimes a political candidate from a minor party has a major influence on an election. Candidates from so-called **third parties** take votes away from candidates from the major political parties. Theodore Roosevelt in 1912 and Ross Perot in 1992 had strong impacts as third party candidates. Their participation took votes away from William Taft and George H.W. Bush. This allowed Woodrow Wilson and Bill Clinton to win those elections. Third parties can also draw attention to important issues that the two main parties ignore. In this way they help bring about change even when they do not win elections.

Which two people were strong third-party candidates in presidential elections?

____

____

CHALLENGE ACTIVITY

Critical Thinking: Making Judgments Which do you believe is better for the United States: a two-party system or a multiparty system? Why?

political party	candidate	two-party system
nominate	political spectrum	multiparty system
coalition	one-party system	third parties
impact		

DIRECTIONS Answer each question by writing a sentence that contains at least one key term from the word bank.

1. What describes the range of political views held by two or more political parties?

____

____

2. In what way does a political party choose the person it wishes to run for office?

____

____

3. In which political system is the ruling party most likely to outlaw parties with an opposing point of view?

____

____

4. Which group might people with similar political views join so that they might help candidates with the same views get elected to government offices?

____

____

5. Leaders from different parties in a multiparty system might form this type of group in order to cooperate and govern together.

____

____

MAIN IDEA

Political parties have workers and committees at the local, state, and national levels. The party nominates candidates for office and campaigns to get those candidates elected.

Key Terms

precincts districts within which all voters vote at the same location

polling place location within a precinct where voting takes place

Academic Vocabulary

distribute to divide among a group of people

Section Summary

PARTY ORGANIZATION

Our political system may seem quite complicated. However, political parties exist for one simple reason: to help elect their own candidates. To do this effectively, they must be well organized. National, state, and local party committees must work toward the same goals. Leaders, committees, and workers have to cooperate. The party must have money to communicate with voters and to support its candidates. For this reason, fundraising is one of the most important activities of a political party.

Identify at least three characteristics of an effective political party.

____

____

____

____

____

The major political parties—and most of the minor parties—have numerous committees. At the national, state, and local levels, these committees plan what the party must do to achieve its goals. The national committee decides on the location and date of the party's national convention. There the party will nominate its candidates for president and vice president. State committees supervise party activities within each state. Again, one of the most important roles is to raise money for the party and for its candidates.

LOCAL ORGANIZATION

Although they get less attention than national political party workers, local party members do very important work. This includes fundraising. Party members also elect local party committee members who in turn serve as local party leaders.

In addition to the divisions we study in geography, each state is divided into voting **precincts**. Within each precinct is a **polling place** where voting takes place. Party committees elect precinct leaders who supervise election workers who communicate with voters. They also organize volunteers who distribute campaign information. Precinct leaders also make sure that voters with disabilities are able to reach the polling place.

What are three important functions performed by precinct leaders?

____

____

____

FINANCING CAMPAIGNS

Political campaigns cost a great deal of money. Candidates for president alone spent nearly one billion dollars in 2004. Fundraising is among the most important activities performed by political parties. Giving money to parties and to candidates is an important way that individuals, businesses, and other groups can influence the government.

The Federal Election Campaign Act (FECA) regulates private political contributions. Presidential candidates may choose to collect public money instead. These funds come from the Presidential Election Campaign Fund. Candidates who accept these funds cannot take private contributions. Often much more money is available from private contributors.

CHALLENGE ACTIVITY

Critical Thinking: Writing to Explore Imagine that you are a precinct leader. Write a short letter to a friend or family member. In it, share your ideas about how to ensure that disabled voters within your precinct will have access to the polling place.

precincts	polling place	distribute

DIRECTIONS Use the three terms from the word bank to write a summary of what you learned in the section.

____

____

____

____

____

____

____

____

DIRECTIONS On the line provided before each statement, write **T** if a statement is true and **F** if a statement is false. If the statement is false, rewrite the sentence to be true on the line.

_____ 1. The place where all voters in a specific district go to vote is called the voting <u>precinct</u>.

____

____

_____ 2. A <u>polling place</u> is where voters within a precinct go to vote.

____

____

Name ______________________ Class ______________ Date ______________

Electing Leaders

Section 3

MAIN IDEA

The right to vote is one of the most important rights held by U.S. citizens. It is the means through which citizens can most directly affect the actions of government.

Key Terms

independent voters voters who are not members of a political party

primary election allows voters to choose candidates for a specific political party

general election allows voters to elect leaders from all political parties

closed primary voters of a specific party choose candidates for the general election

open primary voters from any party choose candidates for the general election

secret ballot a paper ballot listing candidates and marked in private by voters

Section Summary

BECOMING A VOTER

Voting is among our most important rights. Most citizens become eligible to vote upon turning eighteen. The Constitution protects this right. It also guarantees our ability to vote regardless of race, color, or sex. However, these protections do not give us the right to simply show up at a polling place and cast our vote. We must follow certain rules if we wish to vote.

Citizens wishing to vote must register. Registration helps ensure that no other person can vote in our place. It also keeps people from voting more than once in each election. As a part of the registration process, voters are asked to register as a member of a political party. Voters are not required to do so. Citizens can register as **independent voters**. However, in many states, independent voters may be eligible to vote only in certain elections.

The Constitution prohibits restricting the right to vote on the basis of which three characteristics?

____

____

____

ELECTIONS

Most states hold both a **primary election** and a **general election**. Candidates from many political parties appear on the ballot for general elections. However, primary elections vary in which candidates appear on the ballot.

Many states hold what are known as **closed primary** elections. Voters are restricted to choosing candidates who are from their own political party. In this way, voters select their party's candidates for the upcoming general election. These primaries exclude independent voters. Only general elections are open to independent voters in states with closed primary elections. However, some states use **open primary** elections. There, voters of any party—or none—may vote in the primary election. Candidates from all parties may appear on these ballots.

VOTING

Congressional elections take place every two years and presidential elections every four. Candidates' names appear on a **secret ballot**. The ballot is usually paper, although electronic ballots are in use in some places. In either case, voters cast their votes in private.

In many cases voters choose their candidates by voting a so-called straight ticket. They choose only the candidates from their own political party. Others vote what is known as a split ticket. They select the candidates they believe are best, regardless of political party. As a result, their ballots will show selections from both major parties.

How does a straight ticket differ from a split ticket?

____
____
____
____
____

CHALLENGE ACTIVITY

Critical Thinking: Making Judgments Would registering as an independent voter be an advantage or disadvantage during primary elections? Write a paragraph supporting your position.

independent voters	general election	open primary
primary election	closed primary	secret ballot

DIRECTIONS Read each sentence and fill in the blank with the term in the word pair that best completes the sentence.

1. Voters choose leaders from among candidates of both major parties in the ______________________. (general election/primary election)

2. Few states have a/an ______________________, in which voters from any party choose candidates for the general election. (open primary/closed primary)

3. A paper with a list of candidates which a voter uses in private is known as a ______________________. (closed primary/secret ballot)

4. An election in which voters from a specific party choose candidates for the general election is a ______________________. (secret ballot/closed primary)

DIRECTIONS In the space provided, write the letter of the description that best matches each term.

_____ 5. independent voters

_____ 6. primary election

_____ 7. general election

_____ 8. closed primary

_____ 9. open primary

_____ 10. secret ballot

a. election in which all voters choose leaders

b. primary in which voters from all parties choose candidates

c. election in which voters choose candidates for general election

d. primary in which voters of a specific party choose candidates

e. voters not registered with a specific political party

f. paper marked with candidates' names

Name ____________________ Class ______________ Date ______________

Electing Leaders

Section 4

MAIN IDEA

Every four years the United States elects a president. Citizens need to follow the presidential election campaign, stay informed about the candidates and the issues, and vote.

Key Terms

popular vote the vote of the country's citizens

elector person chosen by each state to select the president and vice president

electoral college group of all the electors

electoral votes votes cast by the electors for president and vice president

platform a statement of a political party's views on important issues and policies

plank individual part of a political party's platform

Academic Vocabulary

process a series of steps by which a task is accomplished

Section Summary

THE ELECTORAL COLLEGE

We think of our country as a democracy. However, this does not mean that we vote on each law or on every candidate. As voters we elect representatives who make laws on our behalf. Some of our leaders are elected by **popular vote**. These include state legislators as well as our representatives and senators.

The president and vice president are not elected by popular vote. An **elector** from our state votes for president and vice president for us. Together, these electors are called the **electoral college**. Political parties in each state choose the electors that will represent them in the electoral college.

Members of the electoral college cast **electoral votes** on behalf of the candidates chosen by each state. It is the candidate who wins the majority of

Of all the offices to which we elect leaders, which two are not elected by popular vote?

____

____

the electoral votes—not the majority of popular votes—who wins the presidency.

THE NOMINATION PROCESS

A presidential candidate must first go through the process of becoming a nominee. To win his or her party's nomination the candidate must receive the votes of the majority of delegates at the party convention. Delegates are chosen by political parties in each state and sent to the national convention for this purpose.

The national convention is also where the political party gains attention for its **platform**. This statement of the party's views and policies may help attract new members. Some voters may become interested in a **plank**, or a specific part of the party's platform. Other voters may become interested in a particular candidate.

Primary elections held in each state choose potential nominees for president from each party. As with the electoral college in the national election, the candidate winning the majority of delegates' votes at the convention becomes the nominee for that party. Delegates, along with the presidential nominee, choose the vice presidential candidate for each party.

According to the text, who has the biggest role in choosing a party's presidential candidate? its vice presidential candidate?

____

____

____

____

____

CHALLENGE ACTIVITY

Critical Thinking: Writing to Explore Imagine that you are in charge of the campaign for a political candidate. Construct a platform of four important issues, with a plank for your candidate's position on each issue. You might choose from such issues as the environment, crime, education, healthcare, the economy, or the military.

popular vote	elector	electoral college
electoral votes	platform	plank
process		

DIRECTIONS Answer each question by writing a sentence that contains at least one term from the word bank.

1. What is a statement or list of issues and policies that are important to a political party or to a specific candidate?

____

____

2. Who is chosen to cast a state's votes for president and vice president?

____

____

3. What is the vote of citizens to elect such leaders as senators, representatives, and state legislators called?

____

____

4. What part of a political party's platform includes ideas for dealing with specific issues or policies?

____

____

5. From what group do electors from each state cast votes for president and vice president?

____

____

6. What are votes cast by the electoral college called?

____

____

MAIN IDEA

Political leaders and interest groups find many ways to shape public opinion and influence the beliefs of American citizens.

Key Terms

public opinion total of the opinions held concerning a particular issue

mass media forms of communication that transmit information to large numbers of people

propaganda ideas that are spread to influence people

poll survey intended to measure public opinion

Academic Vocabulary

influence to change, or have an effect on

factor a cause

Section Summary

PUBLIC OPINION AND HOW IT IS SHAPED

The opinions of voters influence how government officials act and work because these officials are employed by the people. If voters are unhappy, they will not re-hire a leader during the next election cycle. Because people hold diverse opinions regarding issues of public interest, political leaders often respond to the majority opinion known as **public opinion** or the total of opinions held concerning a particular issue.

People's opinions are influenced by many factors, including family, friends, experiences, mass media, and propaganda. **Mass media** includes books, magazines, newspapers, radio, television, and the Internet. These forms of communication provide information to large numbers of people. Consumers must understand the difference between fact and opinion when using mass media as a

Circle the factors that influence people's opinions regarding issues of public interest.

source. They must make sure that the information is truthful and reliable before they form opinions.

Some people use the mass media to spread **propaganda,** or information that is intended to influence people to buy something, believe something, or act in a certain way. If propaganda is concealed, makers present information as fact without revealing sources. If propaganda is revealed, makers acknowledge to consumers their intent to influence. In such cases, makers reveal who is financing the message.

How might consumers protect themselves from concealed propaganda?

____

____

PROPAGANDA TECHNIQUES

There are six propaganda techniques. In a testimonial, a famous person supports a product, idea, or person. Someone using the bandwagon technique suggests that a product, idea, or person is popular and trendy. A speaker may use name calling by putting a negative label on an opposing product, idea, or person. A speaker may also use glittering generalities, or words that are positive but meaningless, such as, "I stand for freedom." Speakers may use a plain-folks appeal to suggest that they share commonalities with consumers or voters. Finally, a speaker may use card stacking or an approach that presents only one side of an issue.

Underline the six propaganda techniques.

MEASURING PUBLIC OPINION

To find out about voters' opinions, government leaders and mass media conduct **polls** by asking questions of the public. They try to get a sample that represents the public's opinion on an issue.

Why is it important for pollsters to interview people who represent the public?

____

____

CHALLENGE ACTIVITY

Critical Thinking: Synthesizing Choose an issue important in your school. Design a poll to find out what people in school think about this issue. What questions will you ask to define people's opinions? Whom will you poll to get a representative sample?

DIRECTIONS Look at each set of terms below. On the line provided, write the letter of the term that does not relate to the others.

_____ 1. a. newspaper
b. Internet
c. mass media
d. bandwagon

_____ 2. a. propaganda
b. testimonial
c. magazine
d. card stacking

_____ 3. a. survey
b. poll
c. name calling
d. public opinion

DIRECTIONS Write **T** or **F** on the line to tell whether each statement is true or false.

_____ 4. Public opinion is influenced by mass media and propaganda.

_____ 5. Public opinion is measured by factors.

_____ 6. Propaganda includes plain-folks appeals, radio, and television.

_____ 7. Mass media includes magazines, card stacking, and name calling.

_____ 8. To be accurate, a poll must be based on a representative sample.

MAIN IDEA

Interest groups work to persuade the government to adopt particular policies and address specific issues.

Key Terms

interest groups organizations of people with common interests that try to influence government policies and decisions

lobby an interest or pressure group

lobbyist person paid by a lobby or interest group to represent the group's interests

public-interest groups organizations that promote the interests of the general public

Section Summary

WHAT IS AN INTEREST GROUP?

Americans have the power to influence government policies. One way they do this is by voting. Another way is by forming **interest groups** based on common concerns to influence government policies and decisions. Because an interest group puts pressure on government, it is also called a **lobby.** A **lobbyist** works for an interest group or lobby to represent a group's concerns.

While a political party works to elect its candidates, an interest group focuses on government policies. There are different kinds of interest groups. Some interest groups focus on economic issues that affect businesses or industries, such as the American Farm Bureau Federation. Other interest groups focus on social issues or causes, such as the National Association for the Advancement of Colored People (NAACP). Still other interest groups, called **public-interest groups,** focus on the common good, such as groups that work to protect consumers or the environment.

List two ways that citizens influence government.

____

____

Underline three types of interest groups.

LOBBYISTS INFLUENCE GOVERNMENT

Many lobbyists work in Washington, D.C. Here, they are able to present arguments to Congress in favor of or against policies. For example, a labor group may argue to raise the minimum wage, while a business group may argue against this idea.

Lobbyists use different strategies to promote the interests of their lobbies. In addition to presenting arguments, they may ask members of Congress to sponsor bills. They may conduct research. They may help write bills. They may even provide information regarding public opinion.

Circle five strategies that lobbyists use to influence government.

In addition to influencing Congress, lobbyists may also influence public opinion through paid advertising, election support, and letter-writing campaigns. All in all, lobbyists try to gain public support for their causes, which will influence lawmakers to support legislation for the same causes.

INTERESTS GROUPS AND POWER

As long as interests groups work within the law, they may exert power over lawmakers and the public. The law requires that lobbyists register for whom they work and state how much money is being spent on lobbying efforts. Despite these regulations, some believe that lobbyists unfairly influence government in favor of organizations with large memberships and financial resources. Others view interest groups as an important way for people to participate in government.

Do you think interest groups are a positive aspect of government? Explain.

____

____

CHALLENGE ACTIVITY

Critical Thinking: Making Connections Create a diagram that illustrates the interest groups to which you belong. Consider the roles you play in society and the interests of each group—family member, student, consumer, and so on.

interest groups	lobby	lobbyist
public-interest groups		

DIRECTIONS Use the terms from the word bank to write an e-mail message to a member of Congress in support of a policy that will benefit an interest group to which you belong.

MAIN IDEA

Americans can participate in government by voting and speaking out on the issues that matter to them.

Key Terms

volunteers individuals who work without pay to help others

political action committees groups that collect voluntary contributions from members and use this money to fund favored candidates

Section Summary

FOUR WAYS CITIZENS CAN PARTICIPATE IN GOVERNMENT

A democratic government is based on the participation of its citizens. There are four ways that citizens can participate in government: speaking on public issues, participating in community action groups, voting, and working on political campaigns. To make sure that your voice becomes part of the public opinion on a particular issue, you may "speak" to your congressional representatives and to senators. You can write letters, make telephone calls, and send e-mails or faxes. In addition, you can join community action groups. Such groups often are focused on local issues such as neighborhood improvement, library resources, or park facilities.

Underline the four ways citizens can participate in government.

Circle four ways that citizens may "speak" to Congress.

VOTING IS IMPORTANT

The act of voting allows citizens to participate in government by choosing the officials who will represent the interests of the citizens. In a democracy, voting is a right of citizenship, but it is also an important responsibility. If voter participation is low, then the elected officials represent only a small percentage of the population.

In America, citizens who are 18 years of age may register to vote. However, statistics show that many people do not register to vote. Also, of those who do

Explain how voting is both a right and a responsibility.

____

____

register to vote, many do not cast votes during elections. Citizens have many reasons for not voting: lack of interest, unpopular candidates, illness, travel, and changes of address. One popular reason that people do not participate in the voting process is the belief that their vote does not affect the outcome of an election. However, this is not the case. Each vote works with other votes to reveal who the majority of voters want to lead.

Draw a box around six reasons why people do not participate in the voting process.

TAKING PART IN POLITICAL CAMPAIGNS

If there is a candidate who represents your interests well, you can choose to **volunteer**—at any age—to work on his or her campaign. In addition, interest groups may send volunteers to work on or donate money to campaigns. The law prevents an interest group from donating money directly to a campaign. However, supporters may donate money to **political action committees (PACS)** that may fund candidates. There are more PACs today than there have been in the past. This increase shows the importance of PACs in the political process.

List three causes or organizations that you might support through volunteerism.

____

____

CHALLENGE ACTIVITY

Critical Thinking: Identifying Cause and Effect

Make a chart showing the causes and effects of low voting rates in an election. First, list the reasons that people fail to register to vote. Then, list the effects low voting rates could have on a democracy. Finally, write a paragraph in which you suggest ways to motivate people to vote.

DIRECTIONS Use the space below to create an advertisement for volunteers for a specific organization or cause. Include drawings, charts, or other visual elements as well as text. Include the terms **volunteers** and **political action committees** in the text of the advertisement.

Name ______________________ Class ______________ Date ______________

Paying for Government

Section 1

MAIN IDEA

Each year the local, state, and federal government provide Americans with services such as police, schools, highway construction, and defense. These services cost huge amounts of money. The government pays for these services with taxes collected from citizens.

Key Terms

interest payment made for the use of borrowed money

national debt the total amount of money the U.S. government owes plus interest

revenue money raised from taxes or fees

fees payments charged by governments for various licenses

fine money charged as a punishment for breaking certain laws

bond a certificate stating that the government has borrowed a certain sum of money from the owner of the bond

Academic Vocabulary

primary main, most important

Section Summary

THE HIGH COST OF GOVERNMENT

The cost of running the U.S. government has increased for a number of reasons. The population has grown. The cost of living has increased. The government also provides more services than ever before. Social Security and several health insurance programs make up about half the cost. Defense spending is about a fifth of the budget. Debt also takes up a large amount. The government pays **interest** on money it owes. This interest plus what the government has borrowed is called the **national debt**. This is a payment owed for borrowing money.

Why has the cost of running the government increased?

____

____

THE TAX SYSTEM

Everyone has to pay taxes. Citizens have the right to expect that their taxes will be used wisely. Government officials must figure out which programs need money. They also must think about

Who pays taxes?

____

____

which programs help the most people. Taxes and how they are used is a big debate in our country.

The primary reason why people must pay taxes is to raise money, or **revenue**. Taxes pay for goods and services and the costs of government. They also force citizens to pay more money for some goods. For example, the government places high taxes on cigarettes and alcohol. People are less likely to buy these items because of the higher taxes.

How does the government discourage people from buying certain things?

____

____

The tax system is set up so that citizens should be able to pay their taxes. Taxes are set at different rates. People who make less money pay fewer taxes. Taxes are also applied equally to things that have the same value, such as property. Taxes are also paid on a schedule. This helps people to pay on time. People can also pay late fees and interest if they cannot pay their taxes on time.

OTHER WAYS TO PAY FOR GOVERNMENT

Governments charge **fees** for hunting, driving, and marriage licenses. People using government land or registering their business names or symbols pay fees. A **fine** is a payment for breaking certain laws. Governments also charge for using resources like wood from national forests and electric power from federal dam projects.

If governments need more money, they borrow it. Large projects like bridges and schools require **bonds**. These are promises to pay over a long period of time. Governments pay interest. Those who loan money make money. Voters often have to approve a bond issue. If voters do not approve it, the project will have to be paid for some other way.

Underline the sentence that describes how citizens decide if a bond should be issued for new projects.

CHALLENGE ACTIVITY

Critical Thinking: Predicting Write a newspaper article that might appear in the future about taxes and national debt. How high have they become?

DIRECTIONS Read each sentence and fill in the blank with the term in the word pair that best completes the sentence.

1. Citizens who do not pay their taxes on time have to pay a ______________, which forces most citizens to pay taxes when they are due. (revenue/fine)
2. The more money the government borrows, the more the ______________ increases in total cost. (national debt/bond)
3. When governments borrow money, they have to pay back the ______________, as well as the total amount of the loan. (fine/interest)
4. People or businesses that use land or resources owed by the government pay ______________. (national debt/fees)

DIRECTIONS On the line provided before each statement, write **T** if a statement is true or **F** if a statement is false. If the statement is false, find a word in the word bank that makes the statement true. Write the new sentence on the line provided.

fine	fees	primary

_____ 5. The fine purpose for collecting taxes is to pay for all the services the government provides.

____

____

_____ 6. Governments can make money by forcing citizens to pay fees for licenses to hunt, get married, or drive their cars.

____

____

Name ______________________ Class ______________ Date ______________

Paying for Government

Section 2

MAIN IDEA

Taxes are the main source of revenue for the local, state, and federal governments. The types of taxes each level of government uses to raise money vary.

Key Terms

income tax a tax on what people earn

progressive tax a tax that takes more money from a person with a higher income than it does from a person with a lower income

profit the interest a business has left after paying its expenses

regressive tax a tax that takes the same amount of money no matter how high or low a person's income is

property tax a tax on the value of the property owned by a person or a business

tariff a tax paid on imports, or goods bought from another country

Section Summary

INCOME TAXES

The federal government raises the largest amount of its revenue from the **income tax**. This taxes what people earn from working. The government receives over a trillion dollars in revenue from this tax. The U.S. tax code is a set of laws that controls the taxes that people pay. A person's earnings are one factor in how the tax code determines what taxes are owed.

Why is income tax paid to the government?

____

____

All taxpayers can deduct, or subtract, some of what they earn and not pay taxes on it. This includes deductions for themselves and their dependents. A dependent is often a family member, such as a child. Dependents are exemptions. Their support reduces the taxes that are owed.

Circle the definition of a progressive tax.

____

____

The individual income tax is a **progressive tax**. This means the amount taken from your salary increases or progresses as you earn more. The more a person makes, the more taxes they pay. This type of tax is based on what a person is able to pay.

Employers take income taxes out of paychecks. They send this to the government during the year.

Social Security taxes are also taken from people's paychecks. This money helps those who are retired or unable to work. Most states and some cities take state and local taxes from paychecks. These are lower than federal taxes. Businesses must also pay taxes on their **profits**. This is the income a business has left after paying its bills.

Which taxes are taken from a person's paycheck?

____

____

OTHER MAJOR TAXES

Some states and many cities have a sales tax. This is a charge added to the sale of a product. It is a **regressive tax**. This means that everyone pays the same amount of money. For people who have less income, this tax takes a larger part of their earnings. Excise taxes are also added to some expensive items like air travel and fancy cars.

Why is a regressive tax harder for a poorer person to pay?

____

____

Property taxes allow local government to pay for their services, especially for schools. Owners pay a tax based on the value of property. This includes land and buildings but can also include stocks, bonds, jewelry, cars, and boats.

After a person dies, the heirs may have to pay an estate tax. This is tax on the wealth a person leaves behind. A gift tax also must be paid on gifts that are worth more than $14,000.

The U.S. government collects taxes on products brought in from other countries. This is called a **tariff,** or a customs duty. The government uses these taxes to control the goods that come into our country. It raises the prices of foreign goods. The prices for the same goods made in America are often cheaper.

CHALLENGE ACTIVITY

Critical Thinking: Categorizing Create a chart with two columns. In one row, write a type of tax. In the other, explain what it taxes.

tariff	regressive tax	progressive tax
property tax	income tax	profit

DIRECTIONS Read each sentence and choose the correct term from the word bank to replace the underlined term. Write the correct term in the space provided and then define the term in your own words.

1. A progressive tax makes everyone pay the same amount. It does not matter how much money you earn. ______________________

   Your definition: ____

   ____

   ____

2. Owners of land and buildings have to pay a regressive tax that is based on the amount these things are worth. ______________________

   Your definition: ____

   ____

   ____

3. Income tax that is taken from what a person earns is a property tax. This means the amount paid varies with how much a person earns. ______________________

   Your definition: ____

   ____

   ____

4. A profit is a tax added to the cost of something that is brought over from a foreign country. ______________________

   Your definition: ____

   ____

   ____

Name ______________________ Class ______________ Date ______________

Paying for Government

Section 3

MAIN IDEA

The federal, state, and local governments collect and spend billions of dollars each year. Each level of government has systems to manage public funds.

Key Terms

balanced budget the amount of money coming into the government equals the amount being paid out as expenses

surplus when a government collects more money in revenues than it spends

deficit when a government spends more money than it takes in as revenue

audit a careful examination of financial records by a professional accountant

Section Summary

COLLECTING PUBLIC MONEY

Every level of government has a department that collects taxes. The Internal Revenue Service collects federal taxes. It is part of the Treasury Department. The U.S. Customs Service is another agency of the government. It collects tariffs on goods brought in from other countries. State agencies collect state income taxes. They also collect taxes on a person's wealth after he or she dies. Local tax collectors are responsible for collecting property taxes.

Which agency collects taxes for the federal government?

____

____

State and local governments have a comptroller. This person is responsible for making sure that tax dollars are spent properly. State legislatures or city councils decide how the money will be spent.

SPENDING PUBLIC MONEY

Voters and politicians usually argue about the best way to spend tax money. Governments prepare budgets that list the amount of money collected and where it came from. They also decide how these funds might be spent. Budgets usually cover a period of one year.

Circle the sentences that tell why budgets are important.

The executive and legislative branches manage the money spent in a budget. The president or chief executive creates the budget. The legislative branch has to approve any budget before public money can be spent. The executive branch must then spend the money as the budget allows.

The president needs the help of several government agencies to create a budget. The Office of Management and Budget (OMB) is in charge of this process. The OMB looks ahead and decides how much tax money the government will have. It says what funds will come into the government each year. The heads of the executive departments try to look ahead as well. They decide what funds they will need to do their job. Their requests go to the OMB and the president, who study them. They must decide how much each department will receive.

Which agency helps the president manage the budget?

____

____

The final budget is sent to Congress. The two houses of Congress debate the budget. They approve some items and cut out others. Both houses must approve the budget. An appropriations bill has to be passed to allow the funds to be spent.

Underline the part of government that votes on the final budget.

A **balanced budget** means the government only spends as much as it collects. When more money is collected than spent, there is a **surplus**. These both rarely happen. Usually, more is spent than collected. This is called a **deficit**. The government must then borrow money to make up the difference.

ACCOUNTING FOR PUBLIC MONEY

All levels of government make sure their tax money is properly spent. They conduct an **audit**. This is a careful study of all spending and income by accountants.

Why is an audit important?

____

____

CHALLENGE ACTIVITY

Critical Thinking: Drawing Conclusions Write a letter to the president about all of the things government could do if it had a surplus.

balanced budget	surplus	deficit
audit		

DIRECTIONS Answer each question by writing a sentence that contains at least one term from the word bank.

1. What is it called when governments take in less money than they spend?

____

____

____

____

2. What is the purpose of an audit of government spending?

____

____

____

____

3. Why would people say taxes are too high if there was a surplus?

____

____

____

____

4. Why would a balanced budget make both politicians and voters happy?

____

____

____

____

Name ______________________ Class ______________ Date ______________

Citizenship and the Family

Section 1

MAIN IDEA

From colonial times to today, the American family has changed in many ways. However, the family still plays an important role in teaching young people the lessons that will stay with them for the rest of their lives.

Key Terms

delayed marriage getting married at an older age

remarriage when one or both partners in a marriage have been married before

blended families when one or both partners bring to the marriage children from a previous marriage

two-income families families in which both parents work

single-parent families families that have only one parent

Academic Vocabulary

methods ways of doing something

Section Summary

AMERICAN FAMILIES HAVE CHANGED

The American family has always played an important role in the economic and social history of the United States. Today it remains the backbone of American life and culture.

During colonial times, families were large. People lived on rural farms and produced most of the food and goods they needed to survive. Having many children meant there were more people to help with the work.

Why did people in colonial days have large families?

____

____

____

In the 1800s there was a huge change in how people lived. New inventions and <u>methods</u> of producing goods led to the growth of factories. People left farms and moved to urban areas to work in the factories. People worked long hours to earn money to buy goods that families had once produced on farms. Children also worked in the factories. Often the children worked in unsafe conditions.

CHANGING MARRIAGE TRENDS

Family life greatly changed when families moved to cities. Recently, family life has changed rapidly, especially in marriage trends. **Delayed marriage** is one of these trends. People are waiting until they are older to get married. One reason is that it is more acceptable, today, to remain single. Also many people want to establish themselves in a career before marrying and starting a family.

List one reason why people wait until they are older to get married.

____

____

____

The United States has a high divorce rate. But the rate of **remarriage** is also high. In many of these remarriages, one or both of the parents bring children from previous marriages. Their remarriages create **blended families**, or stepfamilies.

TWO-INCOME AND SINGLE-PARENT FAMILIES

The number of **two-income families** has increased in recent decades. The reason is that the number of women working outside the home has increased. Often it is necessary for women to go to work to add to the family's income. Women, also, now have more career opportunities than ever before.

What is one difficulty single-parent families face?

____

____

____

____

In the past few decades, there has also been an increase in the number of **single-parent families**. These families are formed by a divorce, a death of a spouse, single people adopting children, and births to unmarried women.

All families have difficulties. Single-parent families, however, often have added stresses. It is often difficult for one person to be the only caregiver to a child or children. The income of a single-parent family is often less than that of a family with two working parents.

CHALLENGE ACTIVITY

Critical Thinking: Identifying Write a paragraph identifying and explaining two terms used to describe two types of families today.

DIRECTIONS On the line provided before each statement, write **T** if a statement is true and **F** if a statement is false. If the statement is false, rewrite it on the line provided so that it is a true statement.

_____ 1. Families in colonial times had small families.

____

_____ 2. In the 1800s people moved out of cities to rural areas.

____

_____ 3. New inventions and methods of production led to the growth of factories.

____

_____ 4. The United States has a low divorce rate.

____

_____ 5. People are getting married at a younger age; this is called delayed marriage.

____

_____ 6. Today, the number of two-income families has increased.

____

_____ 7. Remarriages often create blended families.

____

_____ 8. Single-parent families often have many stresses.

____

_____ 9. The rate of remarriage in the United States is low.

____

_____ 10. The family has always played an important economic and social role in American society.

____

MAIN IDEA

U.S. law is set up to protect the well-being of children and families.

Key Terms

family law regulates marriage, divorce, and the responsibilities and the rights of adults and children in the family

child abuse failing to protect a child or acting to cause serious harm to a child

foster home a home in which people agree to take care of a child who is not related to them

guardian a person appointed by the court to take care of a child or an adult who is unable to care for him or herself

adopt when a person not related to a child legally establishes the child as his or her own

divorce legally ending a marriage

no-fault divorce a divorce in which fault is not placed on either partner

Academic Vocabulary

agreement a decision reached by two or more people or group

Section Summary

LAWS REGULATE MARRIAGE

People in families have rights and responsibilities that are protected by laws. **Family law** regulates marriage, divorce, and the relationships between adults and children in families.

Because the needs and customs of families differ in various parts of the country, state legislatures make most laws that apply to families. Some states require a person to be at least age 18 to get married without parental consent. Some require couples to wait a few days after getting a marriage license.

> **What legislatures make marriage laws?**
>
> ______________________
>
> ______________________

Most states require that an official such as a justice of the peace, a mayor, or a judge perform the marriage ceremony. Religious officials of various religions also can perform marriages. All states require witnesses be present to verify that the ceremony was legal.

Recently, the Supreme Court ruled that the Constitution protects a right to same-sex marriage.

LAWS PROTECT CHILDREN

The U.S. government believes children have legal rights. Failing to protect a child or acting to cause serious harm to a child is considered **child abuse.** The state government may place a child in a **foster home** for protection. The parents who abused the child may face criminal charges.

If parents die, a court may appoint a family member or family friend to act as a **guardian**. Sometimes guardians **adopt** the child. If there is no one to be a guardian for a child, the state will put the child up for adoption.

What does the federal government believe children have?

____

____

DIVORCE MEANS DECISIONS

When marriages fail, a couple can seek a **divorce**. Sometimes people charge their partners with desertion or abuse. Usually though, couples seek a **no-fault divorce**. That means the marriage has problems that cannot be resolved.

Couples getting a divorce follow the guidance of lawyers and try to reach an agreement. They agree how the property will be divided, who gets custody of the children, and the visitation rights of each parent. If no agreement is reached by the couple, a judge will decide these issues.

What do couples getting a divorce try to reach before a divorce is granted?

____

____

CHALLENGE ACTIVITY

Critical Thinking: Expressing Point of View Do you agree that children should have legal rights? Write two paragraphs giving your point of view. Be sure to include reasons.

DIRECTIONS Read each sentence and fill in the blank with the term in the word pair that best completes the sentence.

1. ______________________ protect the rights and responsibilities of families. (State laws/Federal laws)

2. Failure to protect a child or acting to harm a child is called ______________________. (child abuse/child adoption)

3. Most states require a person to be at least ______________________ to marry without parental consent. (18/14)

4. ______________________ to a marriage ceremony are required by law in all states. (Witnesses/Entertainers)

5. A ______________________ is a home in which people agree to take care of a child who is not related to them. (safe home/foster home)

6. A person who ______________________ a child not related to him or her is legally establishing the child as his or her own. (adopts/educates)

7. A divorce in which the spouses do not blame one another for the failure of the marriage is called a ______________________. (no-fault divorce/difficult divorce)

8. Couples getting a divorce follow the guidance of lawyers and often reach a/an ______________________. (contract/agreement)

9. Laws that protect the rights and responsibilities of families are called ______________________. (family laws/contract laws)

10. Religious officials of various religions can perform ______________________. (marriage ceremonies/divorces)

Name ______________ Class ______________ Date ______________

Citizenship and the Family

Section 3

MAIN IDEA

The family continues to be the most important group in American society. It performs many functions for its members and for the country.

Key Terms

budget a plan for using money

fixed expenses regular expenses that must be paid usually each month

Academic Vocabulary

influence to change or have an effect on

Section Summary

FAMILY SERVES THE COUNTRY

There are more than 80 million families in the United States. The influence they have on children is huge. Families teach children skills to become responsible adults. Families help keep the United States strong by providing stable homes where children can learn and grow.

Families teach their children basic skills about how to survive. These skills include how to talk, walk, and how to dress.

Children's ideas of right and wrong come from their families. Within the family, children learn how to behave in the world.

Families also teach children how to manage money. Some families give each child a weekly allowance, or a small sum of money. This enables the children to learn how to manage money and become used to financial responsibilities.

Learning to respect the rights of others is also taught in families. In doing so, families teach children how to be good citizens.

List two things families teach their children.

____

____

THE RIGHTS OF THE FAMILY

Many people think of home as a place where a family always lives in harmony. But this is an ideal. Disagreements sometimes happen in families.

Underline the sentence that describes what sometimes happens in families.

How families handle disagreements is important. In a reasonable disagreement, family members learn to respect another point of view. Each family member has rights. If a person's rights are respected, he or she is more likely to respect the rights of others.

Arguments, although unpleasant, can sometimes benefit a family. Disagreements can teach you how to present your ideas effectively. Talking over ideas with members of your family can teach you understanding and patience.

FAMILIES ON A BUDGET

All families have to deal with how to spend their money. Adults earn money to pay for the family's wants and needs. Usually there is only so much money to divide among family expenses.

What can a family do to help make sure the family expenses are met?

____

____

Most families make a **budget**. This can help make sure that the family expenses are met. The starting point of any budget is the total amount of money that is available to spend. Families must spend only up to that amount. If they overspend, they will have to borrow money.

Families must figure their **fixed expenses**. These are expenses that must be paid. Such expenses include housing, food, and electricity. The remaining money pays for things such as health care, transportation, and entertainment. By making a budget, the family can provide for its needs.

CHALLENGE ACTIVITY

Critical Thinking: Summarizing Write two paragraphs that summarize how to make a budget.

DIRECTIONS Look at each set of terms below. On the line provided, write the letter of the term that does not relate to the others.

_____ 1. a. family
b. children
c. parents
d. budget

_____ 2. a. citizenship
b. responsibilities
c. rights
d. arguments

_____ 3. a. budget
b. expenses
c. patience
d. money

_____ 4. a. fixed expenses
b. ideal
c. regular expenses
d. budget

_____ 5. a. influence
b. to change
c. expenses
d. have an effect on

_____ 6. a. disagreement
b. different point of view
c. argument
d. overspend

_____ 7. a. family
b. parent
c. children
d. teacher

MAIN IDEA

Education is vital to American society and to American democracy. The U.S. school system helps prepare you to be a good citizen.

Key Terms

university an institution of higher learning that includes one or more colleges

mainstreaming the practice of treating special needs students like everyone else and teaching them in regular classrooms whenever possible

Academic Vocabulary

values ideas that people hold dear and try to live by

Section Summary

EDUCATION IS IMPORTANT

Education is very important in the United States. The nation has more than 53 million students in grades K–12. More than 3 million teachers work to educate these students. There are two main reasons that education is important. First, it helps individual citizens to grow. Also, education gives all citizens the same chances to learn and succeed. Education is important because it builds a strong country. Young people learn to be good citizens in school.

What are the two main reasons that education is important?

____

____

LEVELS OF THE SCHOOL SYSTEM

The American school system has many levels. Most students will spend at least 14 years in school. This lasts from preschool through high school. Those going on to college and graduate school will spend even more time getting their education.

Beginning with preschool, children then go to kindergarten and elementary school. This is followed by junior high school and high school.

Many of today's jobs require education beyond high school. Higher education includes two main options. The first is community colleges. Students

What is the fewest number of years that most students will spend in the American school system?

____

____

attend these institutions for two years. They can then go right into a job, or finish their studies at a four-year college. Four-year colleges are the second main option for higher education. A college is any four-year institution that offers degrees in many different fields. A **university** includes one or more colleges. Universities also offer advanced studies in many courses. These are known as graduate school. Pursuing higher education gives you more opportunities for your life and career.

What are students' two main options for higher education?

____

____

VALUES AND CHALLENGES OF EDUCATION

Today's schools have become rich, diverse environments. Students study many subjects. They also learn about more than just academics. This has occurred because of basic values of the U.S. education system.

One of these values is that all U.S. citizens receive free public education. This usually lasts from kindergarten through high school. Public education is paid for with money from taxes. Other values include making schooling open to all people. Schools cannot discriminate based on race, gender, religion, or physical disabilities. Treating students with special needs like everyone else, and teaching them in regular classrooms whenever possible, is called **mainstreaming.**

Underline the sentence that explains how the United States pays for public education.

Public schools face a number of challenges today. These include paying for public schools, finding and keeping good teachers, and violence in schools. Everyone must work together to find solutions to these problems. By doing so, students will get the best education possible.

What is one challenge that public schools face today?

____

____

CHALLENGE ACTIVITY

Critical Thinking: Developing Write a brief essay about your career goals and the level of education you will need to achieve your goals.

university	mainstreaming	values

DIRECTIONS Write two adjectives or descriptive phrases that describe the term.

1. university ____

____

2. mainstreaming ____

____

DIRECTIONS Use the vocabulary words from the box to write a summary of what you learned in the section.

____

____

____

____

____

____

____

____

Name ______________________ Class ______________ Date ______________

MAIN IDEA

You can be successful in school if you are aware of the opportunities that your school has to offer and if you are prepared to take advantage of those opportunities.

Key Terms

extracurricular activities the groups, teams, and events that your school sponsors outside of the classroom

Academic Vocabulary

principles basic beliefs, rules, or laws

Section Summary

BE PREPARED, BE SUCCESSFUL

How can you get the most out of school? Making an effort is an important step. By working hard and learning to use your time wisely, you can make the most of your time in school.

Time management means making and keeping a schedule. This skill can help you in two ways. First, you can make sure that everything gets done. Second, you can reduce your stress level. Managing your time means that you will not have any last-minute tasks to worry about.

Underline the sentence that explains the meaning of *time management.*

You can start to make a schedule by figuring out how much time you need for important tasks. These might include homework, after-school activities, and sleeping. You can then use the left over time for fun or relaxation.

What is the first step to take when making a schedule?

____

____

There are many other ways to find success in school. For instance, you should find a quiet, well-lighted place to study at home. You can also learn how to use your textbook to study effectively. In class, you should come prepared with all of your materials. Finish your homework on time, and do not be afraid to ask questions or share your ideas.

When you take a test, look at all of the questions before you begin. Figure out how much time you have to answer each question. Try to leave time to check your work. If a question seems too hard, skip it and move on. Later, you can go back and answer the questions that you skipped.

What should you do when you find a difficult question on a test?

____

____

SEVEN GOALS OF EDUCATION

American schools have seven goals that they want students to achieve. The first goal is to learn basic skills. These include skills such as reading, writing, and computing. Learning to work with others is the second goal. The next goal is to build good health habits. These include eating healthful food, exercising, and having good hygiene. The fourth goal is to train for your life's work. This means learning skills that will help you in your career. Becoming an active citizen is the fifth goal. This means learning about the principles of our democracy, such as community service. The sixth goal is to develop respectful behavior. Using your free time wisely is the final goal of education.

Circle three of the seven goals of education.

EXTRACURRICULAR ACTIVITIES CAN LEAD TO SUCCESS

Taking part in activities outside of the classroom will help you to get the most out of your education. **Extracurricular activities** are the groups, teams, and events that your school sponsors outside of the classroom. For instance, you might take part in a team sport, a school play, or student government. These activities can also help you build skills, meet new friends, and prepare for your future.

What is one way that you can benefit from taking part in extracurricular activities?

____

____

CHALLENGE ACTIVITY

Critical Thinking: Analyzing Think about the ways you prepare for success in school. Identify one of the areas described in this lesson in which you feel you could do better. Then write a plan to help you improve in this area.

DIRECTIONS Use the terms *extracurricular activities* and *principles* to write a letter to a new student who will be moving to your school. Describe in your letter the various extracurricular activities in which students can participate at your school.

MAIN IDEA

One of the key life skills you learn in school should be learning how to think. If you learn how to think critically, you will be able to solve many of the problems you face in school and in life.

Key Terms

experience observation of or participation in events

conditioning learning from the results of our experiences

habit an action we do automatically without thinking about it

motivation the internal drive to achieve your goals

insight thinking that seems to come from your heart more than your mind

creativity the ability to find new ways to think about or do things

critical thinking the thinking we do to reach decisions and to solve problems

prejudice an opinion that is not based on facts

Academic Vocabulary

complex difficult, not simple

Section Summary

LEARNING IS AN EXPERIENCE

Learning is gaining knowledge or skill through study or **experience**. The simplest learning occurs through the experiences of your senses and muscles. For instance, you might have learned from experience that a stove is hot to touch.

Underline the definition of *experience*.

When you touched a hot stove, an adult may have called out "Hot!" The next time you heard this, you probably kept your hand away from the stove. This type of learning is called **conditioning.** Much of our behavior is learned this way. Some behaviors become habits. A **habit** is an action that we do automatically without thinking about it. We learn these by repeating the same actions many times. Other common types of learning include imitation and observing. Imitation means copying the behavior of another person. Observing involves

How do people develop habits?

____

____

What is the difference between imitation and observing?

____

____

taking in information through our senses—by looking, listening, touching, smelling, and tasting.

All people have the ability to learn. But how much you learn depends on you. You must have motivation to learn as much as you can. **Motivation** is the internal drive to achieve your goals. This drive cannot come from other people. You have to develop motivation on your own.

Today's schools allow students to apply many of the different ways that people learn. Schools will teach you to gather information and use it to draw conclusions. Schools today also teach you to work well with others.

LEARNING TO THINK CRITICALLY

The most important skill to learn is how to think. This is a complex process. One way to think is called **insight.** Insight comes from your heart more than your mind. If you have not directly experienced a problem, you can develop insight from experiences with similar situations. **Creativity** is the ability to find new ways to think about or do things. **Critical thinking** is the step-by-step thinking we do to reach decisions or fix problems.

Underline the definition of *critical thinking.*

LEARN TO THINK FOR YOURSELF

The opinions of others often influence our thinking. Thinking critically allows you to look closely at your own opinions. You can think about whether bias or prejudices affect your thinking. **Prejudice** is an opinion that is not based on facts. It can be difficult to be completely free of prejudices. But by trying to do so, you can judge ideas more fairly.

How does thinking critically help you avoid being influenced by prejudice?

____

____

CHALLENGE ACTIVITY

Critical Thinking: Developing Questions Prepare three questions about the different types of thinking and research to answer them.

DIRECTIONS Match the definition with the correct term from the right column.

_____ 1. This is an action that people do automatically without thinking about it.

_____ 2. This term refers to learning based on the results of our experiences.

_____ 3. This is the internal drive to accomplish your goals.

_____ 4. This term describes the observation of or participation in events.

a.experience

b.conditioning

c.habit

d.motivation

DIRECTIONS Read each sentence and fill in the blank with the word or phrase that best completes the sentence.

5. ____________________ is the ability to find new ways to think about or do things. (Insight/Creativity)

6. By remaining free from ____________________ you can judge ideas more fairly. (prejudice/critical thinking)

7. Something that is difficult could be described as ____________________. (insight/complex)

8. ____________________ is the step-by-step thinking we do to reach decisions or fix problems. (Prejudice/Critical thinking)

Name ______________________ Class ______________ Date ______________

Citizenship in the Community

Section 1

MAIN IDEA

There are many kinds of communities. Some are located in transportation centers or farming regions. Others grow where there are jobs in factories or offices. Communities may be small or large, but all of them take advantage of their surroundings.

Key Terms

community a group of people who live in the same area and have common interests

resources the natural features of the land that people may use for living

climate weather

crossroads places where two main roads meet

megalopolis a giant urban area that may form a huge urban chain of cities

Academic Vocabulary

factors causes

Section Summary

FACTORS AFFECTING THE LOCATION OF COMMUNITIES

A **community** is a group of people who live in an area and have common interests. Communities arise for several reasons. One factor that promotes development of a community is the **resources**, or natural features of a place. **Climate**, or weather patterns, also affects the rise of communities. Transportation is another vital factor in the development of communities.

A place with good natural resources attracts people and communities. Good soil helps create farming communities. Fresh water, forests, and other resources attract communities too.

Climate influences communities. A climate that is always warm may lead to the growth of a community based on tourism. Areas with less mild climates may attract communities because they are easily reached by good transportation systems, such

What are two important factors that influence the location of a community?

____

____

as boats (seaport or river), excellent highways, railroads, and so on. Places at a **crossroads**, where two roads or rail lines meet, are often home to thriving communities.

Circle the words that tell what a crossroads is.

TYPES OF RURAL COMMUNITIES

Rural communities contain farms, small towns, and villages. In a rural farm community, most residents work in agriculture. A small country town might arise near a rural farm community. Farmers and other residents use the town's resources, such as its stores, library, and other services.

What are two things you would likely find in a rural community?

____

____

TYPES OF URBAN COMMUNITIES

Cities are urban communities with high population density. About 80 percent of Americans live in urban communities.

Suburbs are less densely populated areas that surround cities. Transportation systems enable people from the suburbs to commute to the city center. Some people like suburbs because they are more open and more like small communities.

Some urban areas have grown so large they have become a **megalopolis**, or giant urban area. A megalopolis may contain cities and suburbs. The area from Boston to Washington, D.C. is considered an Atlantic coast megalopolis.

Circle the words that tell what a megalopolis is.

CHALLENGE ACTIVITY

Critical Thinking: Describing Main Idea In your own words, describe the main characteristic of each type of community discussed in this section.

DIRECTIONS Match the definition with the correct term from the right column.

_____ 1. This is the weather pattern that shapes a given region.

_____ 2. This is a giant urban area that may contain cities and suburbs.

_____ 3. These are surface water, forests, good soil, and other things that may attract and benefit a community.

_____ 4. Criteria, or things that affect what you do.

_____ 5. This is a group of people who live in an area and have common interests.

_____ 6. This is a place where two highways or other types of transportation meet.

a. megalopolis

b. community

c. climate

d. crossroads

e. resources

f. factors

DIRECTIONS Write two adjectives or descriptive phrases that describe each term as it refers to where you live.

7. Community ____

____

8. Resources ____

____

9. Climate ____

____

Name ______________________ Class ______________ Date ______________

Citizenship in the Community

Section 2

MAIN IDEA

People live together in communities for many reasons. Communities provide people with ways to communicate with one another and relax in their free time. Communities also provide services and local governments that help residents make the most of their resources and labor.

Key Terms

communication the passing along of information, ideas, and beliefs from one person to another

public utility one of a group of industries providing services, such as water, gas, and electricity, to both homes and businesses

recreation relaxation or amusement

Academic Vocabulary

efficiently productive and not wasteful

Section Summary

COMMUNITIES TEACH VALUES

People living together in a community should get along. Communicating with others and respect for the law are two values that make getting along easy. Talking with friends, family, and others is a type of **communication**, or a way to share information, ideas, and beliefs with others. When people in a community communicate well, it is easier to solve problems and to respect one another.

What is communication?

____

____

A peaceful community is one in which everyone follows the laws and rules set by the local government. Local government is also a place where people can go to discuss community problems and where neighbors can work together to solve them.

COMMUNITY SERVICES

There are many services a community provides to its residents. These include electricity, telephone services, firefighting, police, and trash services. When community residents cooperate, these services can be provided more efficiently, giving better service at less cost. Providing safety is a main concern of a community. Police and fire departments are supported by the community to ensure citizens' safety.

Schools are another key service provided by a community. Many communities have both public and private schools for child and adult learners.

Public utilities are industries that provide a community with necessary services. These include electricity, telephone service, water, sewage treatment, gas or other heating-fuel distribution, and other important services. Most states regulate utility companies to ensure that they provide good service. In some cases, the local government provides the service.

Circle three services provided by public utilities.

Recreation is an important aspect of any community. **Recreation** is relaxation and amusement. Parks, bike trails, swimming pools, sports teams and stadiums, movies, theaters, skating rinks, bowling alleys, and many other activities are considered recreation. Some recreational facilities, such as neighborhood parks, are free. These facilities are maintained with citizens' tax dollars. Others, such as movies or sports facilities, may charge a fee. Areas with especially good recreational features, such as a beach or snow skiing area, often bring in a lot of money through tourism.

What are two forms of recreation often found in a community?

____

____

CHALLENGE ACTIVITY

Critical Thinking: Predicting What would you predict about the relationship between good communication among neighbors in a community and the quality of life in that community? Explain your answer.

communication	public utility	recreation	efficiently

DIRECTIONS Use all the vocabulary words from the word bank to write a summary of what you learned in this section.

____

____

____

____

DIRECTIONS Look at word at the top of each set of four terms. On the line, write the letter of the term that does not relate to the top word.

_____ 1. Public utility
  a. telephones
  b. drinking water
  c. shopping mall
  d. electricity

_____ 2. Communication
  a. talking to friends
  b. town meeting
  c. visiting neighbors
  d. watching television

_____ 3. Recreation
  a. sleeping
  b. biking
  c. swimming
  d. jogging

_____ 4. Efficiently
  a. costly
  b. easily
  c. cheaply
  d. quickly

MAIN IDEA

Communities provide many benefits and services to their residents. But citizens also need to contribute their energy and efforts if they want their communities to remain welcoming and healthy. Communities depend on cooperation among people.

Key Terms

compulsory required by law

Academic Vocabulary

purpose the reason something is done

Section Summary

HELPING YOUR COMMUNITY

Communities are made up of people. The people in a community can act to make their community a good place to live or a not-so-good place everyone wants to leave. People's actions affect all the communities of which they are a part—from their neighborhoods to their cities, from the nation to the global community of all people.

Your local community provides you with services, such as police, fire fighting, electricity, water, and parks. To keep your community a good place to live, you and all citizens should cooperate and act to improve the community. When neighbors cooperate, they can accomplish a lot to improve their communities and their own lives.

What can you do to keep your community a good place to live?

____

____

Many communities set certain standards of citizenship for all the people who live there. These standards, or rules, are **compulsory**, or required by law. Citizenship standards help to keep the community a good place to live. For example, all citizens must follow traffic laws. In this way they help keep the community's residents safe. Different communities may have different standards, but all are designed to improve community life.

Respecting others in the community is necessary for maintaining a pleasant community. Respecting others is something one volunteers to do. That is, a citizen decides to respect others because it makes life in the community more peaceful and enjoyable.

VOLUNTEERING IS IMPORTANT

Volunteers are important to a community. They help it function and make it a good place to live. People may volunteer to help the sick, elderly, or poor. Some small towns and rural areas have volunteer fire departments and ambulance drivers. Citizens volunteer for these tasks because they want to help their neighbors in the community.

Sometimes a group of volunteers gets together for a specific purpose, or to accomplish a certain goal. Students may join together to volunteer to clean up a park. Some students may volunteer to tutor younger children or to visit the elderly. Retired people often use their time to help others. There are many ways to be a part of volunteer groups.

There are also national groups that depend on volunteers. The United Way, for example, is a national organization that has volunteers working in small local chapters. Whether one volunteers with a national organization or a small group with a specific local purpose, volunteering improves community life. It is also a great way to use your time and to meet new people.

What is one benefit of volunteering?

____

____

CHALLENGE ACTIVITY

Critical Thinking: Categorizing What are some aspects of your community that could benefit from the efforts of volunteers? List as many types of volunteer activities as you can think of. Then arrange your list into categories; for example, education, health, housing, and so on.

DIRECTIONS On the left, list standards of citizenship that you think should be compulsory because each makes life in the community better. On the right, write the purpose of the standard and describe how it improves community life. List as many standards as you can.

Standard	**Purpose**
1. ______________________	______________________
	______________________
	______________________
2. ______________________	______________________
	______________________
	______________________
3. ______________________	______________________
	______________________
	______________________
4. ______________________	______________________
	______________________
	______________________
5. ______________________	______________________
	______________________
	______________________

Citizenship and the Law

Section 1

MAIN IDEA

When a person breaks a law, it is called a crime. There are several types of crimes and a variety of reasons why people commit crimes.

Key Terms

crime any act that breaks the law and for which there is punishment

criminal a person who commits any type of crime

felonies serious crimes, such as murder and kidnapping

misdemeanors less serious crimes, such as traffic violations and disturbing the peace

victimless crimes crimes such as illegal gambling or the use of illegal drugs that do not violate another person's rights but only harm the criminal

white collar crimes nonviolent crimes such as copyright violations, embezzlement, and fraud

Academic Vocabulary

aspects parts

Section Summary

TYPES OF CRIME

When a person breaks the law he or she has committed a **crime**. That person is then known as a **criminal**. The crime may be a **misdemeanor**, which is a minor crime. A criminal may also commit a major crime, such as kidnapping or murder. These serious crimes are called **felonies**. The 29 types of crimes listed by the FBI fall into five main categories. They are crimes against persons and crimes against property. Also included are **victimless crimes**, which are said to only harm the criminal. **White collar crimes** include embezzlement and fraud. Organized crime often provides illegal goods or services.

What are the five main categories of crime?

____

____

____

____

____

CAUSES OF CRIME

There are many reasons why a person might commit a crime. However, some people believe that certain aspects of life in our society lead to crime. Two of the most important are poverty and illegal drug use. When people living in poverty cannot earn enough money, some might turn to crime.

Users of illegal drugs are already criminals. They may commit additional crimes in order to get drugs. Some people believe that increased urbanization also leads to crime. There are other reasons for crime. Often police will find that a person committed a crime for more than one reason.

What are three causes of crime?

____

____

____

____

FIGHTING CRIME

Citizens and the government both have a role in fighting crime. As our population increases, people often live closer together. This makes it more likely that they will be affected by crime. Since the 1990s, the government has made a special effort to fight crime. For example, it has increased the number of police officers. It has also made punishments more severe for serious crimes.

Citizens also take part in fighting crime. They cooperate with the police. Within neighborhoods, residents can watch out for crime and report it. Schools and other institutions can provide education about crime. Even as individuals we can help fight crime by obeying the law ourselves.

CHALLENGE ACTIVITY

Critical Thinking: Writing to Explore Imagine that you serve on a committee of teens and adults in your community. Write a letter to the mayor describing your plan to reduce crime.

crimes	criminals	felonies
misdemeanors	victimless crimes	white collar crimes
aspects		

DIRECTIONS On the line provided before each statement, write **T** if a statement is true or **F** if a statement is false. If the statement is false, find a word or phrase in the word bank that makes the statement true. Write a new sentence on the line provided.

_____ 1. Misdemeanors are committed by people who violate traffic laws.

____

_____ 2. A victimless crime is committed when a person breaks the law.

____

_____ 3. Criminals commit crimes when their lawbreaking harms nobody else.

____

_____ 4. A criminal is someone who commits a misdemeanor or a felony.

____

_____ 5. White collar crimes are minor crimes, such as those committed by motorists.

____

_____ 6. Felonies are major crimes such as murder or kidnapping.

____

_____ 7. Some people believe that certain aspects of American life contribute to crime.

____

MAIN IDEA

Police officers arrest people believed to be breaking the law. An accused person must be tried and, if found guilty, punished.

Key Terms

criminal justice system the three-part system of police, courts, and corrections that is used to keep the peace and bring criminals to justice

probable cause a police officer must have witnessed the crime or gathered enough evidence to make an arrest

arrest warrant an authorization from the court to make an arrest when no witness saw the crime committed

arraignment the hearing at which the defendant enters a plea of guilty or not guilty to the charges he or she faces

acquit what the jury in a criminal case does if they find the defendant in a criminal case not guilty because they had reasonable doubt about the defendant's guilt

plea bargain a defendant may plead guilty to a lesser charge in exchange for a promise of a lighter penalty than a guilty verdict for the original charge

Academic Vocabulary

functions uses or purposes

Section Summary

THE ROLE OF THE POLICE

The **criminal justice system** consists of three parts. Each part has important functions in the fight against crime. The three parts are the police, the courts, and the corrections system. The police arrest people who are suspected of breaking the law.

In order to do this they must have witnessed the crime. They may also gather enough evidence to give them **probable cause**. In some cases they must get an **arrest warrant** from a judge. This means they have convinced the judge that they have probable cause.

What are the three parts of the criminal justice system?

____

____

____

THE COURTS: FROM ARREST TO SENTENCING

The Constitution gives a person who has been arrested the right to a trial. First the court holds a bail hearing. There the judge decides whether the accused person should be released on bail. Next the court schedules an **arraignment**, a hearing in which the defendant pleads guilty or not guilty.

If the defendant pleads not guilty, a trial will be scheduled. If the jury finds the accused guilty, the court will sentence the defendant to punishment. However, if the jury does not believe there is enough evidence for a guilty verdict, they then vote to **acquit** the defendant.

The defendant can also decide to plead guilty. Then there will be no trial. In many cases the defendant and the court will agree on a **plea bargain**. Often this results in a lesser punishment.

PUNISHING LAWBREAKERS

A judge may order a person found guilty of a minor crime to pay a fine or serve a period of probation. Carrying out serious punishment ordered by a judge is the responsibility of the corrections system. One such punishment is imprisonment. Prisons protect society by separating criminals from others.

After imprisonment many criminals serve a period of parole. This supervised release is another form of punishment. The most serious form of punishment provided by the corrections system is capital punishment. Also called the death penalty, it is the most controversial form of punishment provided by the corrections system.

What are the three types of punishment provided by the corrections system?

____

____

____

CHALLENGE ACTIVITY

Critical Thinking: Making Inferences According to the text, most cases in the United States do not go to trial; they are taken care of by plea bargaining. What are some reasons you think this might be the case?

criminal justice system	probable cause	arrest warrant
arraignment	acquit	plea bargain
functions		

DIRECTIONS Read each sentence and fill in the blank with the term in the word pair that best completes the sentence.

1. The court hearing at which a defendant pleads guilty or not guilty is the _____________________. (plea bargain/arraignment)

2. The _____________________ is signed by a judge and gives police permission to make an arrest. (probable cause/arrest warrant)

3. If a jury has reasable doubt about a defendant's guilt it must vote to _____________________. (plea bargain/acquit)

DIRECTIONS Use the vocabulary words from the word bank to write a summary of what you learned in the section.

____

____

____

____

____

____

____

____

____

____

MAIN IDEA

Most states prefer to handle juvenile, or young, criminals differently than adult criminals, but for some crimes this practice is changing.

Key Terms

juvenile in most states, a person under the age of 18

delinquents juveniles found guilty of committing a crime

probation sentence by a judge of a period of time during which offenders must show that they can reform, often by meeting certain requirements such as performing community service

Section Summary

DEFINING JUVENILE CRIME

Many citizens are concerned about crime in the United States. Of special concern is crime committed by children. These young criminals often have fewer opportunities than their peers.

In our society a person under the age of 18 is called a **juvenile**. The criminal justice system calls a juvenile who has been found guilty of a crime a **delinquent**. In 2012 juveniles made up 11 percent of criminal arrests. Most were arrested for larceny or for arson. Many states have created special laws to deal with this growing problem.

For which crimes are the majority of juvenile arrests made?

____

____

____

CAUSES OF JUVENILE CRIME

As with adults, there are many reasons juveniles commit crimes. A recent study identified the most common. They include poor home conditions and poor neighborhood conditions. Researchers also listed gang membership and dropping out of school. The use of alcohol and drugs played an important part, as did peer pressure.

THE JUVENILE JUSTICE SYSTEM

Until the late 1800s juveniles who committed crimes were treated as adults. Today this is true in the case of some very serious crimes. However, special laws apply to juveniles in most cases. These laws protect the rights and privacy of juveniles accused of crimes. They also make it easier for delinquents to get help. This in turn makes it easier for them to lead productive adult lives.

Juvenile court judges have the opportunity to help defendants in their courts. They can order treatment or punishment as they see fit. A defendant who is found guilty of a crime may be sent to foster care. The judge might also sentence an offender to a period of **probation**. If necessary, the delinquent could be sentenced to a stay in a juvenile corrections facility. In other cases a judge may want the offender to have counseling.

A juvenile court judge can sentence a delinquent to which four types of treatment or punishment?

____

____

____

____

AVOIDING TROUBLE

The best course of action for juveniles is to avoid trouble. However, avoiding trouble can be difficult. Following some basic steps will make it easier to stay out of trouble. These include the following:

1. Do not use drugs.
2. Stay in school.
3. Say no to peer pressure.
4. Keep busy with physical activity and hobbies.

These steps will also make it easier to get a good education and to live a successful and happy life.

CHALLENGE ACTIVITY

Critical Thinking: Making Judgments Most states in recent decades have begun trying juveniles as adults, when the juveniles commit very serious crimes. Do you agree or disagree with this policy? Explain.

juvenile	delinquent	probation

DIRECTIONS Use the vocabulary words from the word bank to write a summary of what you learned in the section.

DIRECTIONS Answer each question by writing a sentence that uses at least one word from the word bank.

1. What describes a period during which a juvenile offender can show that he or she can reform?

2. How does the criminal justice system refer to juveniles who have been found guilty of lawbreaking?

3. Which term describes a person under the age of 18?

Name ______________________ Class ______________ Date ______________

The Economic System

Section 1

MAIN IDEA

Countries form many types of economic systems to meet their citizens' needs and wants. The United States has a market economy.

Key Terms

market economy an economic system in which economic decisions are made by people looking out for their own best interests

free market a system that gives people the right to buy and sell goods as they want

profit the money a business has left after it has paid its expenses

scarcity the lack of resources to meet people's wants or needs

law of supply a theory that states that businesses will produce more products when they can sell them at higher prices

law of demand a theory that states that buyers will want a greater quantity of goods when prices are low

free enterprise a system in which business owners may operate with little government interference

capitalism an economic system in which productive resources are owned by private citizens

monopoly when one company sells a product without competition from others

Section Summary

ECONOMIC SYSTEMS

People buy goods and pay for services to fulfill their wants and needs. This process is called the want-satisfaction chain. The details of this process set apart the different economic systems.

There are three types of economic systems: traditional, command, and market. In a traditional economy, people grow their own food, make necessities, and trade with others. In a command economy, the government controls the economy and makes all decisions about production and sales. In a **market economy,** the people own property, start companies, and buy and sell goods within a competitive **free market.**

What is the name for the process of people buying goods and services to fulfill their wants and needs?

____

____

LIFE IN A MARKET ECONOMY

A market economy is based on the desire for **profit,** competition for resources, choice, and supply and demand. Competition for limited resources helps to set prices. When there is a **scarcity** of resources, prices rise and people must make choices about what products to make and buy. The **law of supply** and **law of demand** also set prices. A business will supply more products when it can charge a high price. However, buyers demand more products when the price is low. As prices rise, demand falls. Business owners must find a balance between supply and demand so they can make a profit.

The U.S. market economy is a **free enterprise** system, which means that it operates nearly free from government rules. However, the government does make laws to encourage competition by preventing a **monopoly.** Additionally, within a free enterprise system, business owners, not the government, assume the risk of loss. In a system based on **capitalism,** private citizens own the productive resources, create goods, produce goods, compete with other sellers, and invest in companies.

Why might a monopoly hurt a market economy?

____

____

____

THE U.S. ECONOMIC SYSTEM

Like many countries, our country has a mixed economy because it is a market economy with features of a traditional or command economy. For example, the U.S. government has some regulations to protect people. Our economy is also mixed in the that it has both small and large businesses.

Why might people need government protection from businesses?

____

____

____

CHALLENGE ACTIVITY

Critical Thinking: Comparing and Contrasting

Create a chart with these headings: *Traditional, Command, Market,* and *Mixed.* Then use print and electronic resources to research and list countries with each type of economy. Which type of economy is most popular? Explain.

DIRECTIONS Write two words or phrases that describe each term.

1. market economy ______________________________
2. free market ______________________________
3. profit ______________________________
4. scarcity ______________________________
5. law of supply ______________________________
6. law of demand ______________________________
7. free enterprise ______________________________
8. capitalism ______________________________
9. monopoly ______________________________

DIRECTIONS Study each set of four terms. On the line provided, write the letter of the term that does not relate to the others.

_____ 10. a. market economy
b. free market
c. free enterprise
d. government regulation

_____ 11. a. monopoly
b. law of demand
c. scarcity
d. law of supply

_____ 12. a. productive resources
b. capitalism
c. communism
d. profit

MAIN IDEA

American businesses may be organized as sole proprietorships, partnerships, corporations, or nonprofit organizations.

Key Terms

sole proprietorship a small business owned by one person

partnership a business in which two or more people share the responsibilities, costs, profits, and losses

corporation a large business that is recognized as a separate legal entity

stock shares of ownership in a corporation

stockholders people who buy corporate stocks

dividends corporate profits paid to stockholders

nonprofit organizations groups that provide goods and services without wanting to earn profits for stockholders

Academic Vocabulary

structure the way something is set up or organized

Section Summary

BUSINESS ORGANIZATIONS

In the United States, there are three ways to structure a business: sole proprietorship, partnership, or corporation. A **sole proprietorship** is a small business that is owned by one person. The advantages include total control of the business and its profits. The disadvantages include the owner having to pay all expenses and taxes on his or her own. A **partnership** is a business in which two or more people share the costs, profits, responsibilities, and losses. One advantage is that the partners share the costs and losses. One disadvantage is that the partners may disagree on business decisions. A **corporation** is a large business that is recognized as a separate legal entity. Unlike a sole proprietorship

Circle the three types of U.S. businesses. Then, underline a description of each. Finally, draw boxes around the advantages and disadvantages of each.

or a partnership, a corporation may survive beyond the deaths of its owners.

HOW CORPORATIONS FUNCTION

A corporation raises money by selling **stocks** and bonds. **Stockholders** buy stocks. When a corporation makes a profit, it distributes **dividends** to these stockholders. The stockholders elect directors of the corporation who meet at least once per year to elect a board of directors, vote on issues, and make business decisions. The board of directors selects corporate officers who oversee daily operations. People who buy bonds lend money to a corporation. In return, the corporation repays these loans with interest.

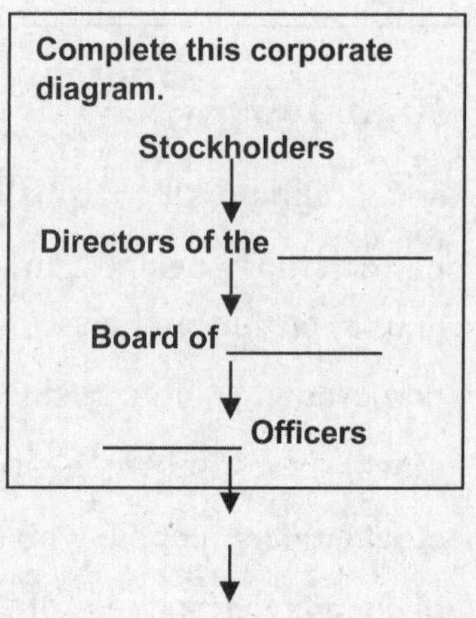

With permission from a state government, a corporation can do business, sell stocks, and receive protection from state laws. In return, a corporation must obey state regulations. If a corporation fails, no one is responsible for the debts. Instead, the property, buildings, and other items are sold to raise money to pay the debts.

NONPROFIT ORGANIZATIONS

Nonprofit organizations provide goods and services without the goal of making a profit for stockholders. They are run by donations. Because they make no profit, they do not pay taxes. However, they may not contribute to political campaigns.

List three nonprofit charities or research, cultural, or education organizations located in your community.

____

____

____

CHALLENGE ACTIVITY

Critical Thinking: Comparing and Contrasting

Create a chart listing the advantages and disadvantages of sole proprietorships, partnerships, and corporations. Then, suppose that you want to open a business based on an interest you have. Write a paragraph explaining which structure you would choose.

sole proprietorship	stock	nonprofit organization
partnership	stockholders	structure
corporation	dividends	

DIRECTIONS Use terms from the word bank to identify and describe each type of business listed below. In some entries, you may use more than one word from the bank.

1. A hair salon owned by one person

____

____

____

2. A music store owned by two people

____

____

____

3. An engineering firm recognized as a separate legal entity

____

____

____

4. The Boy and Girl Scouts

____

____

____

MAIN IDEA

Business owners must make decisions about their use of natural resources, capital, labor, and entrepreneurship. Business owners are free to make these decisions with little interference from the government.

Key Terms

natural resources items provided by nature without human intervention that can be used to produce goods or provide services

capital the manufactured goods used to make other goods or services

labor all human efforts, skills, and abilities used to produce goods and services

entrepreneur a person who organizes, manages, and assumes the risks of a business

Section Summary

FACTORS OF PRODUCTION

There are four factors of production: natural resources, capital, labor, and entrepreneurship. Items from nature, or natural resources, can be used to produce goods or to provide services. **Natural resources** are a factor of production when they requirement payment for use, such as land.

Circle the four factors of production. Then, underline a description of each factor of production.

Capital goods are the manufactured items or services that are needed to make other items and services, such as tools or machines. Financial capital is the money used to buy capital goods. Sources of financial capital include loans, investments, and stocks.

What is the difference between capital goods and financial capital?

____

____

The human efforts, skills, and abilities used to produce goods or services are called **labor.** Workers sell their labor in exchange for fixed or hourly wages or money. The amount of work produced by a worker per hour is called productivity.

An **entrepreneur** is a person who organizes, manages, and assumes the risks of a business. Entrepreneurs take the risks that come with owning a business because they hope to make large profits.

THE GOVERNMENT'S ROLE

One role of government is to help businesses and consumers. To meet these goals, the government sets up regulations to make sure that workers are healthy and safe, buyers are protected, and the environment is safe. In addition, the government makes sure that workers are paid fairly with a minimum hourly wage. It protects workers from being discriminated against by employers. Finally, the government controls competition between small and large businesses. It protects property and trade rights, too.

Underline three services the government provides to workers and consumers. Then draw boxes around three services the government provides to businesses.

Some government agencies aid businesses by helping with planning information, loans, and other forms of assistance. In return for these services, the government taxes business income. This limited government intervention helps ensure that the U.S. economy is strong and healthy.

Some people think that the government should leave American businesses alone. Some government regulations create costs for businesses. These costs are then passed on to consumers through higher prices for goods and services. Government officials and citizens must weigh the advantages and disadvantages of government intervention in business.

List one advantage and one disadvantage of government intervention in business.

____

____

CHALLENGE ACTIVITY

Critical Thinking: Identifying Cause and Effect

Create two cause and effect charts. In one chart, list this cause: *Government Intervention.* Then, list the effects on businesses and consumers. In the second chart, list this cause: *No Government Intervention.* Then, list the effects on businesses and consumers. Based on your chart, write a paragraph stating your conclusions about the role of government in a free market economy.

DIRECTIONS In each column, write at least three examples that match the heading.

Natural Resources	Capital Goods and Financial Capital	Labor

DIRECTIONS Explain the role of entrepreneurs in the nation's economy.

____

____

____

____

____

____

____

Goods and Services

MAIN IDEA

American systems of mass production have made it possible to produce goods more efficiently, which raises the U.S. standard of living. The American economic system has made our economy one of the most successful in the world.

Key Terms

goods things that are made that consumers can buy and own

services things that people do for consumers' benefit

gross domestic product (GDP) the market value or total worth of all things made in the United States during one year

mass production a process of quickly producing large numbers of things that are all the same

profits the difference between the total cost of making something and the total cost received from selling it

Section Summary

WHAT ARE GOODS AND SERVICES?

All the things that are produced by a country's economy are called goods and services. Things that are made are called **goods**. Examples include food, cars, DVD players, buildings, and airplanes. **Services** are things that people do for consumers. Services are not things that consumers buy. Instead, consumers receive a benefit from a service. Doctors, painters, lawyers, and auto mechanics all provide services.

> **What is the difference between goods and services?**
>
> ______________________
>
> ______________________

The total value of all goods and services produced in the United States during one year is called the **gross domestic product** or **GDP**. Economists measure the strength of the U.S. economy by looking at its GDP. Its total is compared to other years. Besides the GDP, economists measure the economy using other factors as well. The number of workers without a job is one factor. The amount of businesses that have failed is another. The dollar amount of taxes collected is a third factor.

MASS PRODUCTION OF GOODS

Our country creates many goods through a process called **mass production**. Machines make the same product over and over again in large numbers. They work faster than humans do. A moving track or assembly line brings parts of an automobile or computer to workers who are responsible for one part of the final product.

Why does mass production lower the costs of making a product?

____

____

THE SERVICE SECTOR

Today, the U.S. economy is sometimes called a service economy. This means that fewer workers make products than provide services. Workers perform personal services on consumers. These may include medical care, haircuts, makeup, and personal fitness. To fix things that are broken, a consumer will use repair services. Repair services can be done on cars, heaters, and air conditioners.

Other types of services are called retail services. Retail services are at shopping malls. They include entertainment services such as movies. Banking, legal work, and insurance are also retail services.

What is the difference between personal and retail services?

____

____

PROFIT, RISK, AND INNOVATION

Our economy is a free market. This means people can take risks to receive a large reward or **profit.** A profit is the difference between their total costs and the amount of money they take in. Businesses that make new products or services can take in big profits.

Circle one effect of a business developing new products and services.

CHALLENGE ACTIVITY

Critical Thinking: Drawing Conclusions Write a paragraph explaining why people take risks to earn a large profit. Explain why this helps to make America's economy successful.

DIRECTIONS Look at each set of terms. On the line provided, write the letter of the term that does not relate to the others.

_____ 1. a. new shoes
b. expensive goods
c. car repair
d. used bikes

_____ 2. a. gross domestic product
b. total sales in one year
c. a measure of the economy
d. retail sales in one month

_____ 3. a. producing a helpful service
b. mass production
c. machines creating products
d. fast creation of products

_____ 4. a. services
b. goods
c. repairs
d. retail

_____ 5. a. expenses
b. costs
c. profits
d. services

DIRECTIONS Read each sentence and fill in the blank with the term in the word pair that best completes the sentence.

6. The ______________________ is a measurement of all the goods and services produced in one year in a country. (gross domestic product/mass production)

7. ______________________ are things people do for consumers that they get paid for. (Services/Goods)

8. The amount of money left over after all the costs of production and selling are subtracted is a company's ______________________. (profit/goods)

9. ______________________ is a process where goods are produced rapidly on an assembly line. (GDP/Mass production)

10. Things that are sold to consumers are called ______________________. (goods/profits)

Name ______________________ Class ______________ Date ______________

Goods and Services

Section 2

MAIN IDEA

Producing goods is only the first step in filling consumers' needs. Getting goods to consumers involves a complex transportation system that makes it possible for American businesses to sell their goods throughout the country and the world.

Key Terms

marketing the process of selling goods and services to consumers

mass marketing the process of selling something the same way to all consumers

Academic Vocabulary

features characteristics

Section Summary

TRANSPORTING GOODS

In the early days of our country, goods were carried on wagons pulled by horses. They were also delivered on boats if there was a river nearby. These ways of transportation were slow. With the first railroads, it became easier to bring goods to market.

Today, railroads and boats still carry goods to market. However, airplanes, trucks, and other motor vehicles provide transportation for goods called freight. Railroads carry bulk or large masses of cargo like coal and grain. Airlines carry goods over long distances. However, airlines carry only 3 percent of the freight shipped. It is cheaper to use railroads or trucks, which carry more for less.

Which methods of transportation carry the most freight for the least amount of money?

____

____

Trucks and vans deliver most goods. A large interstate highway system provides easy access to many markets. A small percentage of goods are still shipped on water. Large container boxes hold goods to be transported on huge ships.

How does a highway system help move goods?

____

____

DELIVERING SERVICES

All types of services, such as entertainment and health care, need to be delivered. They can be delivered in person, over the Internet, through the mail, at retail stores, and even by telephone. Consumers choose services much like they choose goods. They look at the provider's skills, accuracy, and quality of the services they need. Service providers look for ways to attract consumers. They want you to choose them for the service you desire.

MARKETING GOODS AND SERVICES

The process of making goods and services available to consumers is called **marketing**. This is how you convince people to buy your product. **Mass marketing** uses the same product, pricing, and advertising for a product wherever it is sold. Different features have made this type of marketing popular. A one-price system uses a Universal Product Code (UPC), which is read by computers. Self-service allows consumers to buy goods without the added costs of employees helping them. Standard packaging means goods can be delivered at a lower cost.

Draw a box around the different features of mass marketing.

Wholesalers are merchants who do not directly sell to consumers. These distributors transport and store products sold in stores. The Internet has become a fast and easy way to sell and buy products. Fewer stores and employees are needed to market products online. Advertising tries to persuade consumers to buy products. Consumers need to know about a product before they can buy it. Good advertising can make a product successful by giving consumers reasons to buy it.

Underline the role of wholesalers getting goods to consumers.

CHALLENGE ACTIVITY

Critical Thinking: Analyzing Create an advertisement for a new product. Be sure to convince people to buy it!

marketing	mass marketing	features

DIRECTIONS Answer each question by writing a sentence that contains at least one term from the word bank. You may use each term twice.

1. How could someone sell a product to markets all over the world?

____

____

2. What are some of the ways that advertising convinces consumers to buy a product?

____

____

3. What are some of the parts of mass marketing?

____

____

4. How can you tell consumers about a product?

____

____

5. How do self-service, standard packaging, and a one-price system help sell goods to a large number of people?

____

____

6. What characteristics of a product are explained through advertising?

____

____

Name ______________________ Class ______________ Date ______________

Goods and Services

Section 3

MAIN IDEA

As consumers, we learn about the products we buy so that we can make the best choices. Some independent and governmental organizations help protect consumers' interests.

Key Terms and People

consumer a person who buys or uses goods and services

brand a name given by the maker to a product or a range of products

generic product a product that does not have a manufacturer's name or brand

debit card a form of payment that directly takes cash out of a bank account

charge account a form of credit that stores grant to their customers

credit cards a form of payment that allows purchases by lending the consumer money

Section Summary

KEYS TO WISE CONSUMING

A person who buys or uses goods and services is a **consumer**. Good consumers learn when to buy a product. They also find the best place to buy it. Impulse buyers decide quickly to buy something. They may not make the best choice. Wise shoppers look around for the best price and choices.

The **brand** of a product is a name given to it by the manufacturer. Some people only buy brand-name products because they think they are of high quality. A **generic product** does not have a name or brand from its maker. These products usually cost less money. Labels on products give consumers information. This helps them to judge a product. The government requires some information on labels for safety and protection. Many foods have a date for freshness. Labels also list what is in the food or product.

How does the information on a label help consumers with a purchase?

____

____

BUYING ON CREDIT

Credit is any money borrowed when buying a product. This loan has to be repaid later. Cash, checks, or **debit cards** do not involve credit. A check or a debit card takes the money out of a bank account. A **credit card** is another way of paying but it is a loan. You have to pay interest on this loan if you do not pay the bill on time. Some stores offer a **charge account**. This is a form of credit that customers can use to buy things only in that store.

How are credit and debit cards different?

____

____

An installment plan is another way to pay for a product. The consumer pays part of the price of a product. This acts as a down payment. The rest of the amount is paid later. Service charges and interest can add to the total. Credit can cause problems if a consumer cannot pay the debts back.

CONSUMER PROTECTION

Most businesses will work with a consumer if there is a problem with a product. There are also organizations and agencies to help consumers. The Better Business Bureau is a local organization. It helps consumers who feel that they have been treated unfairly. Consumers Union is a private group that tests products. It helps consumers compare products.

Who could help you if you bought a product that did not work?

____

____

The Federal Trade Commission (FTC) watches for false advertising or labeling. The Department of Agriculture makes sure food is safe. The Consumer Product Safety Commission (CPSC) makes sure products are safe. Consumers can also cause problems for businesses through shoplifting and not paying back credit that is owed.

CHALLENGE ACTIVITY

Critical Thinking: Making Inferences Suppose you were planning to buy a video game. Write a paragraph to explain what factors you would consider before making your purchase.

DIRECTIONS Match the term with the correct definition from the right column.

_____ 1. credit cards

_____ 2. brand

_____ 3. debit card

_____ 4. charge account

_____ 5. generic product

_____ 6. consumer

a. something you buy that does not have a brand name on it

b. a name given to a product by its manufacturer

c. someone who buys or uses a product or service

d. a form of payment that is like a check and takes cash from a bank account

e. a form of credit offered by a store to its customers shopping in that store

f. a form of a loan made by a bank to someone making a purchase

Name ____________________ Class ______________ Date ______________

Personal Finances

Section 1

MAIN IDEA

In addition to using dollar bills and coins, individuals and businesses use checks, debit cards, and credit to pay for their purchases.

Key Terms

currency coins and paper money

long-term credit loans payable over long periods of time

short-term credit loans payable within a few weeks or months

bankruptcy a legal declaration that a person or business cannot pay debts owed

creditors people who are owed money

Academic Vocabulary

acquire to get, purchase, or buy

Section Summary

CHARACTERISTICS OF CURRENCY

Currency means the coins and paper money a country uses for purchases. All currency, everywhere in the world, has three common features. First it must be small, light, and easy to carry for everyday use. Second, currency must last a long time and not quickly wear out. Third, it must be a standard form and considered legal tender by the government who issues it.

The Constitution grants Congress the right to issue money and regulate its value. All paper money and coins are legal tender. This means the money is good to pay for goods and services.

List two features currency must have.

____

____

____

CHECKS AND DEBIT CARDS

Today most buyers in the United States make payments for goods and services by check or debit card. To write a check for a purchase, you must have a checking account with a bank. The bank will subtract the amount from your account and pay the

Underline the sentence that compares debit cards to checks.

check. Debit cards are like electronic checks. You pay electronically using your debit card and the money is subtracted from your bank account.

CREDIT AND THE ECONOMY

Credit is a loan of money that is repaid plus interest. Buying something on credit means a person buys something now with the promise to pay for it later. Interest is a payment charged for borrowing money. Stores often issue charge cards that can be used only in that store to purchase goods on credit.

More common is the credit card. It is like a charge card but issued by a bank or credit company and can be used almost anywhere. You present the card when you are purchasing an item, and the store charges the credit card company who pays for it. Then the credit card company sends you a monthly bill. You pay all or part of it. The credit card company charges interest on the unpaid portion.

Who sends a monthly bill to the purchaser for credit card payment?

____

____

____

Credit used wisely can help the average family acquire large purchases like a house. This **long-term credit** means they can get a loan and pay for the house over time. In emergencies, families often get **short-term credit**, which is paid off in weeks. If used unwisely, credit can cause serious problems. If a person cannot make his or her payments on time, he or she might have to declare **bankruptcy.** The courts determine how the person is to pay any **creditors**.

When using credit, what can happen if a person cannot pay his or her payments on time?

____

____

____

BUSINESS CREDIT AND THE ECONOMY

The wise use of credit lets businesses buy and use things before they have saved enough money to pay cash for them. This helps the economy grow.

CHALLENGE ACTIVITY

Critical Thinking: Sequencing Write five sentences sequencing how a credit card transaction works.

DIRECTIONS Read each sentence and fill in the blank with the term that best completes the sentence.

1. Families use ________________ when making a large purchase such as a house or a car. (long-term credit/short-term credit)

2. Few families can afford to ________________ a house without getting a mortgage. (acquire/bankruptcy)

3. People who misuse credit cards will likely have to declare ________________. (creditors/bankruptcy)

4. People who cannot pay their ________________ on time often end up in bankruptcy court. (creditors/long-term credit)

5. For a ________________ to be legal tender, it must be issued by a government. (currency/long-term credit)

6. If used wisely, credit helps us ________________ goods and services before we can pay cash for them. (long-term credit/acquire)

7. In emergencies, families often use ________________. (short-term credit/long-term credit)

8. ________________ issued by the U.S. government can be used in transactions throughout the United States. (Short-term credit/Currency)

MAIN IDEA

Banks provide a safe place to keep money and help businesses and individuals by making loans.

Key Terms

collateral property used to guarantee repayment of a loan

savings and loan associations banks originally established to help people buy homes

credit unions banks that are owned by their members to create a pool of money for low-interest loans

Federal Reserve System (the Fed) established by Congress, it regulates banks by requiring banks keep a certain amount of money in reserve

discount rate the rate of interest the Fed charges member banks that often influences the amount of money available to banks for making loans

discounting the banking process of deducting the interest on a loan in advance

Section Summary

THE ORIGINS OF BANKING

Keeping money safe has been a problem throughout history. Long ago, people took their money to the town goldsmith to hold in secure safes for a small fee. Then the goldsmiths started lending money and charging interest. People would put up **collateral** to guarantee payment of the loans. These practices led to banking.

Why did townspeople take their money to the town goldsmith?

____

____

THE BANKING SYSTEM

Today, businesses and individuals use banks to protect and manage their money. Most people use banks for checking and savings accounts. Money in a checking account is called a demand deposit. The bank must give you your money when you request it. Money in a savings account earns interest. You can also put your money in a time deposit account, called CDs, for a certain amount of time. A money market account usually earns a different interest

Today, what do most people use banks for?

____

____

rate. A NOW account combines checking and savings and it earns interest.

There are four different types of banks. Most banks are commercial banks that offer many banking services. Banking accounts are insured by the government's Federal Deposit Insurance Corporation (FDIC). **Savings and loan associations,** or S&Ls, and savings banks help people buy homes and offer many banking services. **Credit unions** offer a variety of services.

List the four types of banks in the United States.

____

____

____

____

THE FEDERAL RESERVE SYSTEM

When U.S. banks had few rules, some banks failed. To make banks more safe and establish banking confidence, the government established the **Federal Reserve System,** (the Fed) in 1913. The Fed handles the banking needs of the federal government. Twelve district Fed banks regulate banks and require them to keep money in reserve. Banks that borrow money from the Fed pay interest. This rate of interest, or the **discount rate,** influences the amount banks have for making loans.

Identify one reason the U.S. government established the Federal Reserve System.

____

____

GETTING A BANK LOAN

To get a loan from a bank, you explain why you need a loan and give proof that you can pay it back. In giving the loan, the bank transfers the sum, **discounting** interest for the loan. Your loan starts a chain reaction of business transactions. You might buy new equipment from a store that uses the money to pay its employees and suppliers. They then buy goods with the money. Your loan circulates throughout the U.S. economy.

CHALLENGE ACTIVITY

Critical Thinking: Summarizing Design a poster that illustrates how one loan to a business circulates throughout the economy.

collateral	discounting	discount rate
Federal Reserve System	credit unions	savings and loan associations

DIRECTIONS Answer each question by writing a sentence that contains at least one term from the word bank.

1. What did people use to guarantee they would pay back the loan the goldsmith gave them?

____

____

2. What type of bank is owned and operated by its members?

____

____

3. What banks were established to help people buy homes?

____

____

4. What government institution regulates U.S. banks?

____

____

5. What does the Fed charge its member banks for loaning them money?

____

____

6. What is the process called when the bank deducts the interest on a loan when making a loan to an individual or business?

____

____

MAIN IDEA

There are many ways to save money. Saving helps the economy by providing banks with money to make loans to others.

Key Terms

certificates of deposit (CDs) investors invest a certain amount of money for a specific amount of time and get interest on their investment

brokers brokerage house employees who buy and sell stock

stock exchange a market where people buy and sell stocks

mutual funds a fund in which a person owns a small piece of a large number of stocks

money market funds mutual funds that buy short-term bonds that have stable values

Section Summary

SAVING IS IMPORTANT

If you put your money in a savings account, you will earn interest on it. Most Americans save their money in savings accounts. You can withdraw the money when needed. People can also save their money in a **certificate of deposit (CD)** offered by banks and financial institutions. You invest an amount of money for a specified period of time. Interest is paid when that period of time has passed. The longer you save in the CD, the more interest you receive.

Where do most Americans save their money?

____

____

WAYS TO INVEST

You can also invest money in stocks and bonds. A bond is a certificate of debt that a government or corporation gives a person who lends them money. Bonds usually pay interest four times a year. When the bond matures, the lender gets back his or her original investment.

You can also buy stocks or shares of companies through **brokers.** They buy and sell stock for people on **stock exchanges**. The value of stocks depends on the belief of how a company will perform in the future. Stocks, therefore, are a risky investment. If the value of a stock rises, you can sell it at a profit. If the value of the stock falls, you lose money. You should do much research before investing in stocks.

What does the value of a stock depend on?

____

____

Mutual funds are less risky. With these funds, you own a small piece of a large number of stocks. Always research a mutual fund before investing.

You can also put your money in a **money market fund** that buys short-term bonds. You can withdraw your money at any time and the interest paid is usually higher than a savings account. There is some risk, because these funds are not government-insured.

SAVINGS HELPS THE ECONOMY

The money in savings accounts, bonds, and other savings is used to help the U.S. economy grow. Banks lend businesses money to build new factories, hire more people, and purchase new equipment. All this expands the economy.

PROTECTING SAVINGS AND INVESTMENTS

The U.S. government regulates institutions that handle money. The Securities and Exchange Commission (SEC) makes sure stock and bond offerings include accurate information so investors are not misled. The SEC also monitors stock exchanges and brokers. Stocks are still a risky investment, however.

Who regulates institutions that handle money?

____

____

____

CHALLENGE ACTIVITY

Critical Thinking: Listing Make a list of the different ways you can save your money. Include whether each way is safe or risky.

DIRECTIONS On the line provided before each statement, write **T** if a statement is true and **F** if a statement is false. If the statement is false, rewrite the statement on the line to make it true.

_____ 1. Most Americans save their money in cookie jars.

____

_____ 2. Brokers sell certificate of deposits (CD).

____

_____ 3. People can hire brokers to buy and sell stocks on the stock exchange for them.

____

_____ 4. It is less risky to buy shares in mutual funds.

____

_____ 5. Mutual funds buy short-term bonds and the interest earned on the investment is higher than a savings account.

____

_____ 6. The Security and Exchange Commission monitors stock exchanges and brokers.

____

_____ 7. When buying a certificate of deposit (CD), you invest your money for a specific amount of time.

____

_____ 8. You need to do much research before investing your money in a savings account.

____

Name ______________________ Class ______________ Date ______________

Personal Finances

Section 4

MAIN IDEA

Insurance companies offer policies to protect people from possible financial hardships. The federal government also has several programs to help protect people from risks and uncertainties.

Key Terms

insurance a system of protection in which people pay small sums over time to avoid the risk of a large loss

premium the amount you pay for insurance protection

private insurance the voluntary insurance that individuals and companies pay to cover unexpected losses

beneficiary the person named in the life insurance policy who receives the money when the policyholder dies

social insurance government programs meant to protect individuals from future hardship and that individuals and business are required to pay by law

Social Security government system of social insurance

Medicare a federal program of health insurance for people age 65 and older

Medicaid a federal program that helps states pay the medical costs of people with low incomes

Section Summary

INSURANCE PROTECTS YOU

Insurance is a way of spreading risks over large numbers of people. The amount you pay for this protection is a **premium**. Insurance contracts are called policies. Insurance companies take small amounts of money from people and pay them a large sum if a hardship occurs. Not everyone has a hardship, so the insurance company can cover the hardships when they do occur. Insurance companies have reserve funds for when a hardship occurs. State law regulates the size of the fund.

What is insurance?

____

____

____

Voluntary insurance against unexpected losses is called **private insurance**. Life insurance is one kind of private insurance. It protects the family of the policyholder from financial hardship if the policyholder should die. The person named in the policy to receive the money is the **beneficiary**.

Disability insurance provides payments to replace lost wages when a policyholder cannot work because of a disability. Hospital insurance covers medical or hospital costs. Property and liability insurance protects personal property from fire, theft, hurricanes, and vandalism. Car insurance is a kind of property and liability insurance that many have.

INSURANCE PROVIDED BY THE GOVERNMENT

Government programs designed to protect people from hardships are called **social insurance**. Established in 1935, **Social Security** is a government social insurance program with three parts to it. The old-age and survivors insurance is for when people retire. While working, people pay a percentage of their salary each month. When they retire, they receive cash benefits. If they become disabled while working, they can also receive benefits. Employers also contribute to the fund.

What was established in 1935 in the United States?

____

____

Unemployment compensation helps workers who have lost their jobs for reasons beyond their control. Workers compensation helps workers who have job-related injuries or illnesses. It pays medical expenses and helps replace any lost income.

Who does unemployment compensation help?

____

____

The U.S. government also helps poor and older citizens pay their medical expenses. **Medicare** is a federal health insurance program that helps citizens 65 and older pay hospitalizations, some nursing home care, and drug prescriptions. **Medicaid** helps states pay the medical costs of low-income people.

CHALLENGE ACTIVITY

Critical Thinking: Summarizing Write three paragraphs summarizing private and government insurance. Share your work with the class.

DIRECTIONS Read each sentence and fill in the blank with the term that best completes the sentence.

1. ________________________ is a way of spreading risks over large numbers of people. (Premium/Insurance)

2. The ________________________ is the amount you pay for insurance protection. (premium/beneficiary)

3. Life insurance is one kind of ________________________. (government insurance/private insurance)

4. ________________________ are government programs designed to protect people from hardships. (Social insurances/Private insurances)

5. In a life insurance policy the person named to receive the money when the policyholder dies is the ________________________. (beneficiary/premium)

6. Workers who have job-related injuries are helped by the federal government's ________________________ program. (workers compensation/private insurance)

7. The ________________________ government program has three parts to it. (private insurance/Social Security)

8. ________________________ is a government program that helps older citizens pay their medical expenses. (Medicare/Medicaid)

9. ________________________ helps workers who have lost their jobs for reasons beyond their control. (Unemployment compensation/Medicare)

10. The federal government helps states pay for medical care for low-income people in the ________________________ program. (Medicare/Medicaid)

Name ________________ Class ____________ Date ____________

Section 1

MAIN IDEA

The economy has periods of uneven growth called business cycles. Sometimes the economy grows quickly, but other times it may grow very slowly or even shrink. The worst point in the business cycle in the United States was the Great Depression.

Key Terms

business cycle the shifting of the economy from good times to bad and back again

expansion a period of economic growth in the business cycle

inflation a general increase in the price level of goods and services

costs of production the costs of doing business

peak a high point in the business cycle

contraction a period of economic slowdown in the business cycle

recession severe contraction in the business cycle

trough the lowest point of the business cycle

depression a sharp decline in the country's business activity, during which many workers lose their jobs and many businesses close down

Academic Vocabulary

traditional customary, time-honored

Section Summary

THE BUSINESS CYCLE

The shifting of the economy from good times to bad and back again is called the **business cycle.** When the economy grows, this is called **expansion.** Expansion is usually good for the country. Most people have jobs and businesses make money.

However, expansion can cause economic problems such as inflation. **Inflation** is a general increase in the price level of goods and services. During good economic times, people drive up the demand for goods and services. This causes prices to increase. Expansion also causes the **costs of production,** or the costs of doing business, to rise.

What happens during a period of expansion?

____

____

Businesses have to pay more for raw materials, transportation, and workers.

Expansion and inflation stop at the **peak,** or high point, of the business cycle. The economy then begins a **contraction,** or slowdown. When the economy slows enough, a **recession** occurs. The lowest point in a business cycle is called a **trough.** When a trough falls very low, the economy enters a **depression.** Unemployment reaches high levels. Many businesses struggle.

THE GREAT DEPRESSION

The worst depression in U.S. history is called the Great Depression. Beginning in 1929, stock prices fell rapidly. Many banks failed and people lost their savings. Eventually, businesses closed and farm prices fell. Many people lost their jobs and homes.

Circle two consequences of the Great Depression.

Before this time, most economists believed that government should not try to control the business cycle. They thought that problems in the free market would fix themselves. They also believed that recessions could not last long. However, the Great Depression changed these traditional theories.

THE GOVERNMENT'S RESPONSE

During the Great Depression, people became willing to let the government improve the economy. President Roosevelt developed a program called the New Deal. This program took many approaches to solving the nation's economic problems, such as creating many new jobs and restoring people's trust in the banking system and stock market.

How did the Great Depression change the way people felt about government controlling the economy?

____

____

CHALLENGE ACTIVITY

Critical Thinking: Making Inferences Suppose you live in the United States during the Great Depression. Write a journal entry describing the challenges you face. Then explain how government programs might help with those challenges.

business cycle	costs of production	recession
expansion	peak	trough
inflation	contraction	depression
traditional		

DIRECTIONS On the line provided before each statement, write **T** if a statement is true or **F** if a statement is false. If the statement is false, find a word or phrase in the word bank that makes the statement true. Write a new sentence on the line provided.

_____ 1. Inflation is a general increase in the price level of goods and services.

____

_____ 2. Contraction occurs when the economy grows.

____

_____ 3. The high point in a business cycle is called the trough.

____

_____ 4. Costs of production include expenses for raw materials, transportation, and workers.

____

_____ 5. When the economy slows enough, a depression takes place.

____

_____ 6. The shifting of the economy from good times to bad and back again is called the business cycle.

____

MAIN IDEA

Problems such as inflation, unemployment, and recession pose serious challenges to the economy. The government responds to these problems by changing its monetary and fiscal policies.

Key Terms

fiscal policy a government's policy of taxing and spending

monetary policy a government's policy of changing the amount of money in the economy

Academic Vocabulary

policy rule, course of action

Section Summary

CAUSES OF ECONOMIC PROBLEMS

Economic problems such as inflation, unemployment, and recession are serious problems facing our economy. Economists identify a number of factors that cause these problems.

> **What are some of the major problems facing our economy?**
>
> ____________________
>
> ____________________

One such cause is the money supply. When the economy has too much money in circulation, inflation results. Inflation also happens when financial institutions loan too much money. When there is too much money to spend, this drives prices higher. Government spending can also cause inflation because it puts more money into the economy.

> **Underline three ways in which the money supply can cause inflation.**

Productivity is the amount that a worker produces in an hour. Increases in productivity often lead to higher wages, higher profits, and lower prices. Recently, productivity in the United States has begun to trail that of other nations. As a result, foreign goods have often become less expensive than goods produced in the United States.

GOVERNMENT'S RESPONSE TO ECONOMIC PROBLEMS

The U.S. government can respond to economic challenges in a number of ways. One of these ways is by changing its **fiscal policy,** or policy of taxing and spending. For instance, suppose the economy is entering a recession. The government might lower taxes and increase its spending. These steps could provide relief to citizens and create new jobs.

Circle the definition of *fiscal policy.*

In a recession, the government might also use **monetary policy,** or a change in the money supply. The Federal Reserve System (the Fed) controls the nation's money supply. The Fed might increase the money supply in response to a recession. It could also invest money in banks to improve the flow of credit. When inflation gets too high, the government might raise taxes. The Fed might also raise the reserve requirements. These steps reduce the money supply.

How would the Fed likely respond to a recession?

____

____

OTHER WAYS TO HELP THE ECONOMY

Fiscal and monetary policies alone cannot keep the economy healthy. Government, consumers, and businesses can take additional steps to improve the economy.

For example, government can reduce wasteful spending and stop unneeded programs. Consumers can spend less and save more of their income. They can also help U.S. businesses by buying American-made products. Finally, business managers and workers can try to improve their productivity.

What steps can consumers take to improve the economy?

____

____

CHALLENGE ACTIVITY

Critical Thinking: Comparing Make a chart that shows how fiscal policy and monetary policy are alike and different.

DIRECTIONS Use the terms **policy, fiscal policy,** and **monetary policy** to write an email message to your friend explaining what you learned in this section.

Name ______________________ Class ______________ Date ______________

MAIN IDEA

Workers formed labor unions to force employers to improve working conditions and wages. Businesses and unions have had conflicts over the years, so the federal government passed laws dealing with labor relations.

Key Terms

labor unions organizations of workers formed to demand better conditions from their employers

collective bargaining negotiation between labor and management

strike a negotiation method in which union members walk off the job if employers do not agree to labor's demands

picketing walking back and forth, often carrying signs, in front of company buildings

job action any type of slowdown or action short of a strike

mediation a method of settling disputes in which an expert examines the issue and recommends a solution

arbitration a method of settling disputes in which an expert arbitrator makes a binding decision

Academic Vocabulary

contract a binding legal agreement

Section Summary

THE RISE OF FACTORIES

Work in the United States began to change with the start of the Industrial Revolution. Many people began to work in large factories with difficult conditions. Workers faced long hours and received low wages. There were very few safety laws. Many workers faced injuries and even death.

When did work in the United States begin to change?

____

____

THE RISE OF LABOR UNIONS

As American industry continued to grow, many workers became unhappy with these conditions. They formed groups called **labor unions.** Labor unions demanded better conditions. These groups wanted things such as higher pay, safer working conditions, and shorter workdays.

Union leaders worked to achieve these goals through **collective bargaining,** or negotiation between labor and management. Representatives from both sides look to find a compromise. When they reach an agreement, its terms go in a contract.

Labor leaders used a variety of methods to respond when employers refused to cooperate. In a **strike,** union members walk off the job. Strikers often use **picketing** to prevent others from doing their jobs. Picketers march in front of company buildings, often carrying signs. Rather than striking, workers can also simply work much slower than usual. This is called a slowdown. Any such action that falls short of a strike is called a **job action.**

Underline examples of improvements to working conditions that labor unions demanded.

What are two methods that labor leaders used to respond when employers refused to cooperate?

____

____

LABOR LAWS

Conflicts between labor and management became violent during the late 1800s. Political leaders began to pass laws to bring the two sides together. Laws such as the National Labor Relations Act help the two sides work together peacefully.

Why did U.S. political leaders begin to pass labor laws?

____

____

LABOR TODAY

Disputes do still occur today. Both sides usually work to settle these disputes through collective bargaining. At times, though, they need help to resolve their differences. In **mediation,** an expert examines the dispute and recommends a solution. Both sides then evaluate the expert's ideas. In **arbitration,** an expert arbitrator makes a decision that is binding on both sides.

CHALLENGE ACTIVITY

Critical Thinking: Elaborating Write and perform a dialogue between labor leaders and employers about a labor issue from early American industry.

DIRECTIONS Read each sentence and fill in the blank with the term in the word pair that best completes the sentence.

1. Union leaders worked to achieve their goals through ____________________, or negotiation with management. (collective bargaining/job action)

2. An expert's decisions are binding on both sides in ____________________. (mediation/arbitration)

3. Workers attempt to block other people from taking their jobs through ____________________. (contract/picketing)

DIRECTIONS Write two adjectives or descriptive phrases that describe the term.

4. labor unions ____

5. collective bargaining ____

6. strike ____

7. job action ____

8. mediation ____

Name ______________________ Class ______________ Date ______________

The U.S. Economy and the World

Section 1

MAIN IDEA

In a market economy, buyers and sellers interact in the marketplace and respond to changes in prices by changing the amounts demanded and the amounts supplied.

Key Terms

consumer a person who buys goods or services

producer a person or company that provides goods or services

circular-flow model a model that describes how individuals, households, businesses, and government interact in the economy

competition the economic rivalry among businesses selling similar products

Academic Vocabulary

development creation, as of a new product

Section Summary

BASIC ECONOMIC SYSTEMS

There are three basic economic systems. In a traditional economy, economic decisions, such as distribution of goods and services, are based on customs and traditions. In a command economy, government officials determine the production and distribution of goods. In a market economy, the interactions among producers and consumers determine what is produced and how it is distributed. A mixed economy includes elements of two or more basic economic systems.

> **Who makes economic decisions in a command economy?**
>
> ______________________
>
> ______________________

THE FREE-ENTERPRISE SYSTEM

Under the free-enterprise system, such as that in the United States, individuals have the right to own private property and to choose how to use it. In this type of economy, consumers and producers affect how the system works. A **consumer** is a person who buys goods or services. A **producer** is a person or company that provides goods or services.

> **What do we call a person who provides a good or service?**
>
> ______________________
>
> ______________________

The **circular-flow model** shows the interaction among individuals, households, businesses, and government that shapes the economy. In the model, goods, services, and resources move in one direction, while money moves in the other direction.

Circle the words that tell what the circular-flow model shows.

Supply and demand are key to the free-enterprise system. Supply and demand affect prices. If many people want a rare good, that good's price is high. If few people want an abundant good, that good's price is low. If many people want a good, producers may make more of it. As the good's supply grows, its price declines and more people buy it.

Competition is the economic rivalry among producers selling similar products. Competition may lead producers to make better, cheaper products to attract consumers.

Circle the words that tell what competition is.

INVESTMENT AND THE ECONOMY

Some people invest their money in stocks. A stock represents a partial ownership in a company. If the company does well, the stockholder makes money.

New businesses seek venture capital to grow. This is money given to a new business to help it get off the ground. It is "seed" money that helps the company develop its new product or service.

Many established companies spend some of their profits on research and development. Development is inventing and perfecting new products.

There is always risk in investing. A stock price may fall if profits shrink. A small business may not develop a sellable product. Development may not yield a good, new product.

What is the purpose of development?

____

____

CHALLENGE ACTIVITY

Critical Thinking: Analyzing Create a graph or flow chart that shows the relationship between supply, demand, and price.

consumer	competition	development
circular-flow model	producer	

DIRECTIONS On the line provided before each statement, write **T** if a statement is true and **F** if a statement is false. If the statement is false, write the correct term on the line after each sentence that makes the sentence a true statement.

_____ 1. The two children's toy companies engaged in competition to make the best and most popular toys.

____

_____ 2. A company engages in research and competition to create new products to sell.

____

_____ 3. The supply and demand model shows the economic interactions among individuals, households, businesses, and government.

____

_____ 4. Most of the time, a producer shops for and buys the best product at the lowest price.

____

_____ 5. A doctor is a consumer because he or she offers a service to people.

____

_____ 6. Government participation is part of the circular-flow model in economics.

____

MAIN IDEA

Sometimes the economy performs well. Sometimes economic activity is not as strong. Many factors affect the performance of the economy. Economists try to understand how the economy is doing and predict its direction in order to advise businesses and the government.

Key Terms

leading indicators factors that come before a major change in the business cycle

coincident indicators signs that show economists how the economy is doing at the present time

lagging indicators economic signs or factors that follow a change in the business cycle

Section Summary

THE BUSINESS CYCLE

The business cycle is the repeated series of periods of expansion and contraction of the economy. There are four stages in the business cycle: expansion, peak, contraction, and trough.

Several factors influence the business cycle. An important factor is how much businesses invest in capital goods and increased production or new equipment. The availability of money and credit also affects businesses' ability to grow. The public's expectations about the economy affect people's behavior, such as consumption, which affects business. Finally, international events affect businesses all over the world.

What economic indicator tells economists about the present condition of the economy?

____

____

Economists try to predict changes in the business cycle. They look at one of three types of indicators, or signs, that reflect the condition of the economy. **Leading indicators** are signs that come before a change in the economy. The number of building permits issued is a leading indicator of what will happen in the economy.

A **coincident indicator** is a sign that shows the condition of the economy at the present time, or at the time the economists are analyzing it. Coincident indicators, such as people's salaries, tell economists if the economy is on an upturn or downturn.

Lagging indicators follow, or lag behind, a major economic change. A lagging indicator tells economists how long an economic phase may last. The unemployment rate is a lagging indicator. Unemployment may remain high even while the economy is improving.

HUMAN AND CAPITAL RESOURCES

Human resources are people, or workers. Capital resources are money, raw materials, equipment, and other real goods. Capital resources may come from anywhere. Increasingly, human resources are being accessed from around the world. For example, many U.S. companies open factories in Asia where wages are low. To increase profits, businesses seek capital goods from countries where they are sold most cheaply. They also try to reduce their labor costs by hiring low-wage workers.

What are human resources?

____

____

CURRENT EVENTS AND THE ECONOMY

Current events, such as wars, terrorist attacks, natural disasters and other major events also affect the economy. For example the September 11 attacks shut down the New York Stock Exchange and severely hurt the airline industry. Hurricane Katrina and the BP oil spill in the Gulf of Mexico hurt the local economy. They also hurt the national economy as oil prices skyrocketed.

What are two types of current events that affect the economy?

____

____

CHALLENGE ACTIVITY

Critical Thinking: Predicting What type of economic indicator is unemployment? What would you predict about how the unemployment rate changes as the economy moves from a severe contraction to moderate expansion? Explain your answer.

coincident indicator	lagging indicator	leading indicator

DIRECTIONS List the terms from the word bank in the order in which they tell what is happening with the economy. Then write one or two examples of each type of indicator.

1. This indicator predicts what will happen in the economy. ______________

   Examples of this indicator: ______________________________

   ____

2. This indicator tells what the economy is doing now. ______________

   Examples of this indicator: ______________________________

   ____

3. This indicator changes after the economy begins to change. ______________

   Examples of this indicator: ______________________________

   ____

Name ________________________ Class ______________ Date ______________

The U.S. Economy and the World

Section 3

MAIN IDEA

The government affects the economy through regulation and policy, the Fed through fiscal monetary policy. Proper use of these tools helps keep the economy functioning more smoothly and effectively.

Key Terms

tax incentives special tax reductions that help lower a company's tax bill if it follows certain policies the government favors

easy-money policy a policy that increases the growth of the money supply

tight-money policy a policy that reduces the growth of the money supply

open-market operations the buying and selling of government bonds

reserve requirement the amount of money banks must have available at all times

Section Summary

GOVERNMENT REGULATION

All levels of government regulate business. Regulations are for protecting workers, protecting consumers, limiting negative effects, encouraging competition, and regulating property.

Government regulations prevent businesses from using workers in unsafe or unfair ways. Government regulations protect consumers by overseeing the safety of consumer products. Government regulations limit negative effects on the environment from economic activities, including regulations to minimize pollution. The government has also passed laws to promote competition. Antitrust laws break up huge businesses that limit competition from smaller firms. Finally, the government regulates how certain property can be used. For example, zoning regulations prevent land from being used in harmful ways.

List three goals of government regulations.

____

____

____

FISCAL POLICY

Government fiscal policy—how it gets and spends money—influences the economy. Governments raise money through taxes, and tax policy affects the economy. For example, during a recession taxes may be lowered to spur consumption. Government may also offer businesses **tax incentives**, special tax reductions for businesses that follow certain government policies, to promote economic activity.

Circle the phrase that explains what a tax incentive is.

Government spending affects the economy. When the government buys more goods and services, it pumps money into and stimulates the economy. The government may also provide public transfer payments, such as unemployment insurance, to help people buy goods and services.

MONETARY POLICY

The Federal Reserve controls the amount of money in circulation. During a recession, the Fed may use an **easy-money policy** to increase the money supply and stimulate the economy. When there is inflation, the Fed may prefer a **tight-money policy**, which reduces the money in circulation.

What does the Fed buy and sell in open-market operations?

____

____

Open-market operations involve the Fed buying or selling government bonds. For example, selling bonds lowers the money supply because the money people put into the bonds is not spent on other things. The Fed also uses banks' reserve requirement, or how much money banks must have available, to control the money supply. If the Fed requires a high reserve, there is less money circulating. Lowering the reserve increases the amount of money in circulation. Whatever policy the Fed uses, timing is vital. The Fed's actions must address economic conditions in a timely manner.

CHALLENGE ACTIVITY

Critical Thinking: Making Inferences What do you think the U.S. government and the Fed may do to stimulate economic growth in the U.S. economy? List several things each can do that influence the economy and can encourage growth.

DIRECTIONS Match the definition with the correct term from the right column.

_____ 1. These are tax breaks given to businesses that follow certain government policies.

_____ 2. This is a Fed policy that increases the amount of money in circulation.

_____ 3. This is the amount of money banks must have available at all times.

_____ 4. This is a Fed policy that reduces the amount of money in circulation.

_____ 5. This Fed activity involves the buying and selling of government bonds to alter the amount of money in circulation.

a. reserve requirement

b. tight-money policy

c. open-market operations

d. tax incentives

e. easy-money policy

DIRECTIONS Write at least two policies that government can use in each of the following economic conditions.

6. There is a recession and government must stimulate the economy.

____

____

7. There is inflation and government must reduce the amount of money in circulation.

____

____

The U.S. Economy and the World

MAIN IDEAS

International trade allows countries to specialize in producing the goods and services where they are most efficient. Trade gives people access to more goods and services. Trade also makes countries interdependent.

Key Terms

absolute advantage when a nation can produce more of a product than another country

comparative advantage when a nation can produce a product more efficiently than another country

opportunity cost the value of the next best alternative that is given up when a nation specializes

trade barrier a limit on the exchange of goods

balance of trade the difference between the value of a nation's imports and exports

trade surplus when a nations sells more than it buys

trade deficit when a nation buys more than it sells

Academic Vocabulary

agreement a decision reached by two or more people or groups

Section Summary

WHY NATIONS TRADE

Nations trade to get goods and services they otherwise would not have. For example, the United States imports coffee. Trade makes nations interdependent.

Nations specialize in producing and selling certain goods. A nation has an **absolute advantage** when it produces more of a given product than another country. A nation has a **comparative advantage** when it can provide a product more efficiently. Efficiency arises from a lower **opportunity cost**, which is the value of the next best alternative that is given up when a country specializes.

Circle the phrase that tells the meaning of "absolute advantage." Underline the phrase that defines "comparative advantage."

FREE TRADE VERSUS PROTECTIONISM

A **trade barrier** limits the exchange of goods. It is a form of protectionism. Trade barriers include tariffs, or charges on imports; quotas, which limit the amount of an imported product; and voluntary restrictions, which are agreements by nations to limit trade in some way. An embargo is an extreme action that bans all trade with another nation.

Most nations favor trade, and cooperate to promote it. There are several types of trade agreements: those between nations, those involving a whole region, and those that include many world nations. For example, NAFTA is a regional trade agreement intended to promote free trade.

Generally, protectionism hurts national economies because it may lead to price increases or trade wars. Most countries' policies mix free trade with some protectionism for certain industries.

What are two types of trade agreement?

____

____

THE VALUE OF TRADE

International trade has a system for valuing the currencies of different countries. A foreign exchange market determines the value of each currency compared with others.

Trade has a strong effect on the economy. A nation's **balance of trade** is the difference between the value of its imports and its exports. If a nation exports more than it imports, it has a **trade surplus**. If it imports more than it exports, it has a **trade deficit**. The United States imports far more than it exports, so it has a large trade deficit.

Trade surpluses and trade deficits are two different conditions in what aspect of a nation's economy?

____

____

CHALLENGE ACTIVITY

Critical Thinking: Evaluating Why would too much protectionism depress an economy? Is there such a thing as too much free trade? If so, how might too much free trade harm a nation's economy?

agreement	comparative advantage	opportunity cost
balance of trade	trade surplus	absolute advantage
trade deficit	trade barrier	

DIRECTIONS Read each sentence. Choose a term from the word bank to fill in the blank and correctly complete the sentence.

1. Several African countries have a(n) ______________________ in the production and export of coffee, which they produce more of than any other countries.
2. Placing a high tariff on one type of imported product is a type of ______________________ that reduces trade.
3. Because the United States imports more goods than it exports, it has a large ______________________.
4. The ______________________ is the value of the next best alternative that is given up when a country specializes.
5. The World Trade Organization is a type of international ______________________ to promote free trade among member nations.
6. China is a nation that exports far more than it imports, so its ______________________ is quite large.
7. The ideal for a nation is to have a fairly even ______________________ in which imports and exports are more or less the same.
8. A nation has a(n) ______________________ when it can produce a product more efficiently than other nations.

Name ______________________ Class ______________ Date ______________

Foreign Policy

Section 1

MAIN IDEA

The United States has relationships with many foreign countries. Both the president and Congress play roles in conducting foreign policy.

Key Terms

alliance an agreement in which two or more countries commit to help each other

executive agreement a mutual understanding between the president and the leader of a foreign government

diplomatic recognition power of the president to recognize or establish official relations with a foreign government

diplomatic corps U.S. ambassadors to foreign countries and their assistants

Academic Vocabulary

aspects parts

Section Summary

GOALS OF U.S. FOREIGN POLICY

Countries establish working relationships with each other through foreign policy plans. The goals of U.S. foreign policy are to maintain national security, support democracy, promote peace, provide aid to people in need, and establish open trade.

Underline the five goals of U.S. foreign policy.

THE PRESIDENT'S POWERS

According to the Constitution, the president, who leads the nation's foreign policy, has powers in three areas: military actions, treaties, and diplomacy. As commander in chief, the president may order military action. However, Congress must approve any action that goes beyond 60 to 90 days. Also, only Congress has the power to declare war.

Draw a box around the president's three areas of power with regard to foreign policy.

With two-thirds approval from the Senate, the president has the power to make three types of treaties: peace, **alliance,** and commercial. A peace treaty ends a war. An alliance treaty establishes an agreement between two countries to help each other. A commerical treaty establishes a trade agreement. In addition, the Constitution gives the president the power to establish an **executive agreement** with a foreign leader. This agreement is not a treaty, but an understanding.

What does a treaty do?

____

____

Additionally, the president can establish official relations with another country through **diplomatic recognition.** The two countries exchange ambassadors and assistants, who form a **diplomatic corps** to represent the interests of their countries.

THE FOREIGN POLICY BUREAUCRACY

In addition to others, three important government agencies contribute to U.S. foreign policy: Department of State, Department of Defense, and the Peace Corps. The Department of State, headed by the Secretary of State, advises the president and supervises U.S. ambassadors. The Department of Defense, headed by the Secretary of Defense, advises the president on military matters. Both the president and the Department of Defense receive information from the Joint Chiefs of Staff. The Peace Corps, a volunteer program, provides assistance in areas such as education and farming. It also promotes cultural understanding.

What government agency advises the president on military matters?

____

____

CONGRESS PROVIDES A BALANCE

In addition to the power to declare war, Congress influences aspects of foreign policy through committee recommendations, treaty approval, and spending approval in the area of defense.

With regard to foreign policy, list the powers of Congress.

____

____

____

CHALLENGE ACTIVITY

Critical Thinking: Analyzing Write an essay explaining how technology, trade, and travel make the world a smaller, more interdependent place than it once was. Make sure to include a discussion of the increasing importance of foreign policy.

DIRECTIONS Read each sentence and fill in the blank with the term that best completes the sentence.

1. A(n) _______________ is an understanding the president makes with a foreign leader. (executive agreement/treaty)

2. The president can establish official relations with another country through _______________. (treaty-making powers/diplomatic recognition)

3. The Department of State supervises the activities of the U.S. _______________. (diplomatic corps/Congress)

4. The president has the power to make _______________ treaties with nations who want to help each other in areas such as defense, economy, or science. (alliance/commercial)

DIRECTIONS Write two words or phrases that describe each term.

5. alliance ____

6. executive agreement ____

7. diplomatic recognition ____

8. diplomatic corps ____

9. aspects ____

MAIN IDEA

To promote peace and stability, the United States engages in diplomacy with other nations. These alliances with other countries serve mutual defense, economic, and other needs.

Key Terms

diplomacy the process of conducting relations between countries

summit a meeting between the leaders of two or more countries to discuss issues of concern

foreign aid any government program that provides economic or military assistance to another country

balance of trade the difference in the value between a country's exports and imports over a period of time

Section Summary

DIPLOMACY AND ALLIANCES

As chief diplomat, the president meets and talks with leaders of other countries. Some of the goals of **diplomacy** are preventing war, ending conflict, solving problems, and setting up communication. To reach these goals, a president may go to a **summit** or State Department officials may travel to other countries.

Underline the four goals of diplomacy.

To promote peace, our country forms defense alliances. For example, the United States is a member of the North Atlantic Treaty Organization (NATO), which is made up of non-communist nations. In addition, our country belongs to alliances with Latin American and Pacific Rim countries.

FORMS OF FOREIGN AID

The United States provides material, economic, or military **foreign aid** to countries in need of help after a war or natural disaster. This is part of our country's foreign policy.

ORGANIZATIONS PROMOTE FOREIGN TRADE

Foreign trade is an important part of U.S. foreign policy. To have a strong economy, our country must make more money from its domestic exports than it spends on foreign imports. The difference between the money spent on these is the **balance of trade.** In recent years, the United States has had large trade losses. Competition from Pacific Rim countries in the areas of automobiles and technology is one reason for this loss. A single currency (the euro) established among European countries is another.

What must our country do to have a strong economy?

____

____

Trade agreements can help fix this imbalance. For example, the United States set up free trade agreements with countries in North America and in Central America. Our country hopes to make better trade agreements with Pacific Rim countries too.

To monitor international trade, many countries belong to the World Trade Organization (WTO). In addition, the United Nations World Bank and the International Monetary Fund (IMF) lend money to countries in need. These loans support free-market economies. The United Nations (UN) is also involved in setting up global environmental standards for industry to protect air and water, limit global warming, protect endangered species and their habitats, and find alternative energy sources.

How does the United Nations World Bank try to promote a safe international free market economy?

____

____

Some Americans do not support international free trade agreements. They fear the loss of jobs and industries and foreign competition. Others believe that free trade will help the U.S economy grow.

CHALLENGE ACTIVITY

Critical Thinking: Synthesizing Write a trade agreement proposal between the United States and a Pacific Rim country such as Japan. Think about what rules of trade will benefit both countries.

DIRECTIONS Answer each question and provide an explanation.

1. Which two countries need diplomacy—two countries in conflict over a trade agreement or two countries in agreement over a border dispute?

2. Who might attend a summit—a group of tourists or the leaders of two or more countries?

3. Which country is in need of foreign aid—a country that has been hit by a tsunami or a country that has received a normal amount of rainfall?

4. Which country does **not** have a favorable balance of trade—the one that spent more money on imports than it made on exports or the one that made more money on exports than it spent on imports?

MAIN IDEA

The United Nations provides a forum in which countries may discuss serious problems and work toward solutions.

Key Terms

United Nations an international organization that promotes peaceful coexistence and worldwide cooperation

General Assembly the UN body that discusses, debates, and recommends solutions to problems

Security Council the UN body that is mainly responsible for peacekeeping

International Court of Justice the UN law court, also known as the World Court

Section Summary

THE UNITED NATIONS

After World War II, fifty world leaders met to form the **United Nations** (UN). Member countries make the following pledges: to save future generations from war, live in peace as good neighbors, and protect basic human rights.

Underline the three pledges UN member nations must make.

Today, the UN, headquartered in New York City, has 193 permanent members. It is divided into six parts: General Assembly, Security Council, International Court of Justice, Trusteeship Council, Economic and Social Council, and Secretariat. The **General Assembly** discusses, debates, and recommends solutions to problems. It meets one time per year, and each member country gets one vote. A two-thirds majority of the Assembly decides important issues.

How are majority votes in the U.S. Congress and the UN General Assembly alike?

____

____

____

The **Security Council** has 15 members. Five of these are permanent members and 10 are temporary members. All are elected by the General Assembly for two-year terms. If countries are in conflict, the Security Council may recommend diplomacy or military force. Fifteen elected judges in the **International Court of Justice** decide legal matters, such as boundary disputes or debt payments. The Trusteeship Council, which no longer exists, helped colonies without self-government at the end of World War II.

The Economic and Social Council does studies and makes recommendations in the areas of health, human rights, education, drugs, and population. The Secretariat manages the day-to-day operations of the UN. Also, the UN maintains specialized independent agencies such as the World Health Organization (WHO).

To which UN council or agency would you like to belong? Explain.

____

____

____

THE UN IN THE MODERN WORLD

The UN provides a place where all the countries in the world may work together to promote peace, health, and prosperity. Ideally, the UN supports diplomacy in times of conflict. However, while the UN does not have a military, it maintains a peacekeeping force to monitor conflicts. Peacekeepers may use their weapons only to protect themselves.

Some Americans criticize the UN. They say that it is expensive to maintain. Some think it cannot enforce peace without a UN army. Others believe that voting that does not favor powerful nations over other weaker nations. However, other Americans support the UN as the best hope for world peace.

List the arguments in favor of and against the UN.
For:

____

____

Against:

____

____

CHALLENGE ACTIVITY

Critical Thinking: Applying Think about the U.S. Pledge of Allegiance. What is its purpose? What promises do Americans make when they recite it? Now, create a pledge for nations who want to become a member of the UN. What is the purpose of this pledge? What promises should member nations make? Perform your pledge for the class.

DIRECTIONS Complete the diagram to show the structure of the UN.

UNITED NATIONS

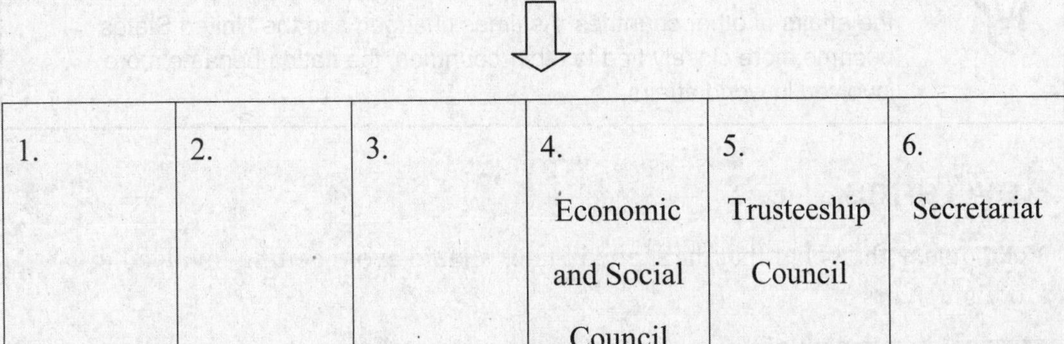

1.	2.	3.	4. Economic and Social Council	5. Trusteeship Council	6. Secretariat

INDEPENDENT, SPECIALIZED AGENCIES

World Health Organization and Others

DIRECTIONS Fill in the blank and then write down the responsibilities of each of its six parts.

The ______________________ is an organization that promotes peace and worldwide cooperation.

1. ____

2. ____

3. ____

4. ____

5. ____

6. ____

MAIN IDEA

For many years, U.S. leaders shaped a foreign policy to avoid involvement in the affairs of other countries. As times changed and the United States became more closely tied to other countries, the nation became more involved in world affairs.

Key Terms

isolationism the belief that the United States should avoid getting involved in foreign affairs

doctrine a statement of policy that sets forth a way of interacting with other countries

corollary a statement that follows as a natural or logical result

dollar diplomacy the practice of sending U.S. troops to other countries to protect U.S. investments

neutrality a policy of not favoring one side or the other in a conflict

Academic Vocabulary

consequences the effects of a particular event or events

Section Summary

INDEPENDENCE AND ISOLATIONISM

After America won its independence, it faced problems at home. Most government leaders supported **isolationism.** They did not want to get involved with other countries' problems.

Britain and France were at war in Europe in the 1790s. Many Americans supported one side or the other. In 1793, President George Washington issued the Neutrality Proclamation. This stated that in a war America would not take sides.

Later on, there were conflicts with the British colony of Canada. British and French ships were also seizing U.S. ships in the Atlantic Ocean. The War of 1812 brought the United States into war against Britain. Neither side won but there were positive consequences, such as increased patriotism

Why did government leaders believe in isolationism after the Revolutionary War?

____

____

____

____

and respect from other countries. For almost 100 years, America avoided European wars.

THE UNITED STATES AND INTERNATIONAL RELATIONS

Many countries in Latin America won their independence from Spain in the early 1800s. President James Monroe wanted to protect that independence. He declared that the U.S. would consider any European interference an unfriendly act. This policy became known as the Monroe Doctrine. This **doctrine** became a guide for U.S. foreign policy for years. In 1904, President Theodore Roosevelt strengthened the doctrine, with the Roosevelt Corollary. A **corollary** is a statement that follows as a natural or logical result.

How was the Monroe Doctrine a warning?

____

____

____

Roosevelt stated that if Latin American countries had problems, the U.S. would help them. This foreign policy became known as **dollar diplomacy**. The U.S. protected money that businesses had invested in Latin America and sent in troops to keep the peace. Many Latin American countries felt they were being oppressed. In 1933, the Good Neighbor Policy was announced, which stressed friendly agreements.

WARS END ISOLATIONISM

When World War I began in Europe in 1914, President Woodrow Wilson declared a policy of **neutrality**. Then German ships attacked U.S. ships, and America declared war in 1917. The League of Nations was formed after the war to keep countries out of war. It failed. After World War II, the United Nations formed to keep the peace among nations.

What was the purpose of the League of Nations?

____

____

____

CHALLENGE ACTIVITY

Critical Thinking: Making Judgments In your opinion, should the U.S. avoid getting involved in the affairs of other countries? Why or why not?

dollar diplomacy	isolationism	doctrine
neutrality	consequences	corollary

DIRECTIONS Read each sentence and choose the correct term from the word bank to replace the underlined phrase. Write the term in the space provided and then define the term in your own words.

1. President Monroe issued a neutrality that guided U.S. policy in Latin America for many years. ______________

   Your definition: ______________________________

   ____

2. After the Revolutionary War, government leaders favored dollar diplomacy.

   ____

   Your definition: ______________________________

   ____

3. The United States used corollary to protect American business interests in Latin America. ______________

   Your definition: ______________________________

   ____

4. Consequences in foreign wars means that the United States would not support or help either side. ______________

   Your definition: ______________________________

   ____

5. President Roosevelt strengthened the Monroe Doctrine when he added a neutrality. ______________

   Your definition: ______________________________

   ____

MAIN IDEA

The United States and the Soviet Union worked together during World War II, but the two nations became rivals soon after the war ended. Their political rivalry turned into a competition for global power that became known as the Cold War.

Key Terms

communism an economic system in which the government controls what is produced

satellite nations countries controlled by another country

containment the U.S. foreign policy of preventing the spread of communism

balance of power a situation in which countries are about equal in strength

limited war a war fought without using a country's full power, especially nuclear weapons

détente a term for relaxing and calming down tense relations between countries

Academic Vocabulary

strategies plans for fighting a battle or a war

Section Summary

CAUSES OF THE COLD WAR

After World War II, a Cold War began. The United States and the Soviet Union believed in different economic systems. Both countries struggled to control other countries without fighting a real war.

The Soviet Union had a system called **communism**. In this system, the government controls the economy and resources. Individuals are not allowed to own factories, farms, or businesses. The Communist Party ruled with an iron fist. It crushed opposition to the government.

The countries along its borders became **satellite nations**. The Soviets controlled them. The United States joined with other noncommunist nations to gain world power and influence. Both the United

What does the government control in a communist system?

____

____

____

____

States and the Soviet Union used strategies such as spying and foreign aid to "win" the Cold War.

THE POLICY OF CONTAINMENT

In 1947, President Harry S. Truman announced that the U.S. would give economic aid to countries that were fighting against communism. This is called the Truman Doctrine. The idea behind this policy was to prevent communism from spreading, or **containment**. The United States wanted to stop communism and keep the Soviet Union from occupying other countries. The Berlin Blockade tested this policy. The Soviet Union tried to block anyone and anything from coming into Berlin. The United States and Britain sent airplanes with food and supplies to Berlin. The Soviet blockade failed.

What was the purpose of the policy of containment?

____

____

____

In 1949, Communists gained power in China and Cuba and later in North Korea and North Vietnam. The Soviets supported these governments. They also showed the world they had nuclear weapons when they built missile bases in Cuba. The Soviet Union and the United States now had a **balance of power**. To try to contain communism, the United States fought a **limited war** in Vietnam and Korea. No nuclear weapons were used to fight the wars.

THE END OF THE COLD WAR

The Soviet Union spent too much money during the Cold War. Its economy was failing. Soviet leader Mikhail Gorbachev offered **détente** as a solution. This easing of tensions between the United States and the Soviet Union helped lead to the fall of communism. In 1991, the Soviet Union broke apart. The Cold War was over.

Underline the name of the policy that helped lead to the end of the Cold War.

CHALLENGE ACTIVITY

Critical Thinking: Evaluating Write a paragraph about how the world would be different today had communism not fallen in the Soviet Union.

détente	satellite nations	balance of power
strategies	limited war	containment
communism	strategies	

DIRECTIONS Use six of the words or phrases from the word list to write a summary of what you learned in the section.

____
____
____
____
____
____
____
____

DIRECTIONS Look at each set of terms below. On the line provided, write the letter of the term that does not relate to the others.

_____ 1. a. communism
b. government control
c. limited war
d. ownership of resources

_____ 2. a. Cold War end
b. fall of Soviet Union
c. détente
d. balance of power

_____ 3. a. détente
b. satellite nations
c. spread of communism
d. containment

_____ 4. a. balance of power
b. Soviet republics
c. limited war
d. Cold War

Name ____________ Class ________ Date ________

Charting a Course

Section 3

MAIN IDEA

A primary goal of U.S. foreign policy has been to promote peace, trade, and friendship throughout the world. In the face of terrorism, war, and ongoing conflict in the Middle East, the United States and other governments have had to take a more aggressive approach to foreign policy in recent years.

Key Terms

terrorists people who use violence against civilians to achieve political goals

War on Drugs an organized effort to end the trade and use of illegal drugs

embargo a government order forbidding trade

World Trade Center a business complex in New York City that was destroyed by a terrorist attack on September 11, 2001

Pentagon the headquarters of the U.S. military leadership

Northern Alliance an Afghan group that had fought against the Taliban since the early 1990s

Academic Vocabulary

facilitate to bring about or to help to make something happen

Section Summary

GLOBAL CONFLICTS

After the end of the Cold War, Russia transitioned to a free-market economy. Some former Communist countries joined NATO. A major goal of the United States and its allies is to stop terrorist attacks. **Terrorists** use violence against civilians to achieve political goals. When ethnic conflicts broke out in the former Yugoslavia, NATO helped achieve a peace settlement there in 1995.

What caused the United States to lead an attack on Iraq in the 1990s?

____

____

____

In 1990, Saddam Hussein, the ruler of Iraq, invaded Kuwait. America led an international force against Iraq and freed Kuwait from Iraqi control. In 2003, U.S. forces invaded Iraq and overthrew Hussein, who was seen as a threat to world peace.

Israel is a state that was created after World War II in the Middle East. Arab nations opposed Israel

How did creating new countries lead to conflicts in the Middle East and India?

____

____

and fought wars against it as a result. The United States helped Israel reach peace agreements with Egypt and Jordan. Another conflict simmers between India and Pakistan. Both nations were created when India became independent in 1947. Recent efforts have eased tensions, but both countries possess nuclear weapons.

GLOBAL POLITICS AND TRADE ISSUES

In Africa, a civil war in Somalia broke out in the early 1990s. In the Darfur region of Sudan, fighting forced millions of people to leave their homes.

U.S. foreign policy in Latin America and Canada has opened new markets and trade. The **War on Drugs** has been an organized effort to end the trade and use of illegal drugs. Cuba remains the only Communist country in Latin America. The United States has eased an **embargo,** or government order forbidding trade, with Cuba to promote change.

9/11 AND THE WAR ON TERROR

On September 11, 2001, Islamic terrorists used hijacked airplanes to attack the **World Trade Center** and the **Pentagon**. Thousands of people were killed in the attacks. The U.S. government then launched a war on terrorism. The Department of Homeland Security was created to protect against future attacks.

Evaluate the U.S. government's response to the 2001 terrorist attacks.

____

____

____

Osama bin Laden, the leader of al Qaeda, had ordered the attack. The United States and its allies attacked Afghanistan, where al Qaeda was based. The **Northern Alliance**, an Afghan group, aided the fight. U.S. forces later found and killed bin Laden.

CHALLENGE ACTIVITY

Critical Thinking: Summarizing List three reasons for some of the conflicts you read about in this section. What caused these problems?

War on Drugs	Northern Alliance	embargo
Pentagon	World Trade Center	Terrorists

DIRECTIONS On the line provided before each statement, write **T** if a statement is true and **F** if a statement is false. If the statement is false, rewrite it as a true statement on the line.

_____ 1. Terrorists are people who attack civilians to achieve their political goals.

____

_____ 2. The Northern Alliance helped to fight terrorists in Afghanistan.

____

_____ 3. The World Trade Center is the headquarters of the U.S. military.

____

_____ 4. The War on Drugs has attempted to stop the sale and production of illegal drugs in Latin America.

____

_____ 5. The embargo against Cuba has been eased to help promote change.

____

_____ 6. The Pentagon is a group of buildings in New York City that terrorists attacked on September 11, 2001.

____